SINGING

Susan Sutherland

TEACH YOURSELF BOOKS

For UK orders: please contact Bookpoint Ltd, 39 Milton Park, Abingdon, Oxon OX14 4TD. Telephone: (44) 01235 400414, Fax: (44) 01235 400454. Lines are open from 9.00 – 6.00, Monday to Saturday, with a 24 hour message answering service. Email address: orders@bookpoint.co.uk

For U.S.A. & Canada orders: please contact NTC/Contemporary Publishing, 4255 West Touhy Avenue, Lincolnwood, Illinois 60646 – 1975 U.S.A. Telephone: (847) 679 5500, Fax: (847) 679 2494.

Long-renowned as the authoritative source for self-guided learning – with more than 30 million copies sold worldwide – the *Teach Yourself* series includes over 200 titles in the fields of languages, crafts, hobbies, sports, and other leisure activities.

British Library Cataloguing in Publication Data
A catalogue record for this title is available from The British Library

Library of Congress Catalog Card Number: 95-68144

First published in UK 1995 by Hodder Headline Plc, 338 Euston Road, London NW1 3BH

First published in US 1995 by NTC/Contemporary Publishing, 4255 West Touhy Avenue, Lincolnwood (Chicago), Illinois 60646-1975 U.S.A.

The 'Teach Yourself' name and logo are registered trade marks of Hodder & Stoughton Ltd.

Copyright © 1995 Sue Sutherland.

Typeset by Transet Limited, Coventry, England.
Printed in Great Britainf for Hodder & Stoughton Educational, a division of Hodder Headline Plc, 338 Euston Road, London NW1 3BH by Cox & Wyman Ltd, Reading, Berkshire.

Impression number   10 9 8 7 6 5
Year   2004 2003 2002 2001 2000 1999 1998

— ACKNOWLEDGEMENTS —

My mother was able to do things with her voice that I, as a very small child, had not thought possible. As a trained singer making music in our house, she grabbed my attention and aroused an interest that has stayed with me and continued to develop throughout my life. She has always encouraged and nurtured that interest and I thank her for it.

A sincere 'thank you' to everyone who has supported this project at Hodder and Stoughton Educational, allowing me to share my great love for singing, and music in general, with a wider audience: Helen Coward, Sue Hart, Sarah Mitchell and Rowena Gaunt deserve special mention. Helen went as far as trying out some of the physical exercises as she travelled to work on the train, much to the alarm of her fellow passengers, no doubt!

I have been fortunate indeed in having Sue Bettaney, dear friend and accomplished musician, to play piano accompaniments on the cassette, and I couldn't possibly mention the cassette without thanking Rowan Laxton, the sound engineer, whose patience and good humour made the day a memorable one.

Using my voice effectively began when I was eleven. My splendid choir mistress, Edna Jamieson, of the Maia Choir, Stockport, gave me a sound grounding in musical education and imparted her unbounded enthusiasm for musical excellence and enjoyment of choral music. I was further encouraged by, Miss Holt, my school music teacher who, 'hoped her little candle would throw her beams far', and Edward Paine, my piano teacher, who set my sights on the Royal Manchester College of Music.

Sylvia Jacobs, my singing teacher at the Royal College, introduced me, kicking and screaming, to the concept of discipline. There may have been a delayed reaction, but I can assure that excellent teacher that her words *were* heeded... eventually.

I was then taken under the wing of the late Frederic Cox, O.B.E., Principal of the Royal College, who had more faith in me than I had in myself.

Anthony (Tony) Rooley, Director of the Consort of Musicke, master lutenist, and inspirational visiting tutor at the University of York, opened my mind to new ideas and approaches; and Peter Seymour, my tutor at York, made me strive to match his own rigorous standards.

Very special thanks indeed must go to Stephen Wilkinson, formerly Director of the BBC Northern Singers, who is simply the best choral director. Though unrelenting in his quest for superlative performance, Stephen was most generous in spirit and certainly the greatest fun to work with.

My husband, Steve, and children Sara, James and Leonie, are all musical in their different ways and wise enough to recognise that we all march to a different beat. Happily, we manage to play in concord most of the time. Without their love and support, there would be no book.

In memory of my father, Leopold Mosco,
who loved a good tune.

CONTENTS

INTRODUCTION

'Since singing is so good a thing
I wish all men would learn to sing.'

William Byrd, 1588

Singing is not just for the specialist, it is for everyone to enjoy. *You* are an instrument, waiting to be played. If you are lucky enough to possess a naturally beautiful voice, have the confidence to use it and are eager to improve your skills and stamina, this is the book for you. If you don't think yourself quite so lucky, read on! It draws upon the proven methods and experience of a long line of fine singers and teachers. The exercises and ideas you will find here are the rightful heritage of everyone who wants to make music with their voice.

If you were praised and encouraged to sing as a small child, the chances are that singing will come as naturally to you as speech. If, on the other hand, you were told to keep quiet and mime, probably for no better reason than your voice was louder than anyone else's, take courage. You may say you're tone deaf, but young children learn to speak by listening and copying and they learn to sing in exactly the same way... if they are encouraged to do so.

Are you the child that was told to mime? Maybe you had a powerful voice which you had not learned to modulate. Other children in your group might have had voices the size of a pea, but they sang out, so you copied, only to find your voice roared above the rest. Many children, who go on to be creditable singers, have to be helped to sing in tune, so those pea-sized voices may not have been any more accurate than your own, but they couldn't be heard as well, could they?

Using the techniques in this book, you will learn to listen and discriminate, skills which will enable you to produce a more accurate and appealing sound.

If you would love to sing and have a full and confident speaking voice, but find that your singing voice emerges as a hoarse whisper, the chapter Confident Projection is for you.

You may be wondering whether or not this book is relevant to your type of singing. Can a 'classical' foundation provide the right sort of basis for a rock, cabaret, folk singer, etc., to build upon? The answer is yes. First find your *basic* voice. A voice that is your ambassador in sound. Exercise that voice regularly until it is a robust and dependable instrument. When you have developed vocal fitness and control, you can direct your voice along a path of your own choosing.

In *Teach Yourself Singing* you will find exercises that nurture and develop your voice instrument, whether you want to sing solo, in a group, as an amateur or as a professional. Together with building the foundation of a sound singing technique, you can expect, over time, to develop better posture, a keen and discriminating musical ear, secure presentation skills and growing self-confidence. You will be able to throw away your inhibitions. You would think nothing of learning a new language, a skill that requires study, listening and practice. Music is a language and singing allows us to be the instrument through which that language is spoken, sometimes expressing emotions too deep for words.

All it takes is a commitment to spend a little of your time each day 'working out', vocally speaking. If you wanted to become physically fit, you would expect to use your muscles in a carefully planned programme of exercise and you wouldn't expect instant results. Training the voice isn't so different; patience is the touchstone, so record the progress of your work and keep your expectations reasonable. When you hear an improvement, treat yourself to a CD or a trip to a concert. Make the occasion a bench-mark in your study that spurs you on to the next goal.

The surest way to reach that first level of achievement is to listen carefully to every sound you make. Sing, listen, sing again. Teach your ear to be discriminating as you build up your skills and don't settle for second best. Hear that special sound in your mind, the sound you would like to make, then *go for it!* Listen to great singers, singing great music, but don't worry about whether you will ever sound like one of your particular idols, you are the first and only you.

You cannot imagine the pleasure in store. Plato himself believed in the mystical potency of song, saying 'Songs are spells for souls...'.

HOW TO USE THIS BOOK

The book has been written in three parts: Part One includes breathing, posture and relaxation exercises to prepare the body physically; Part Two, the lesson plans, covers various styles of song, and each plan has a list of objectives; Part Three offers practical advice on, for instance, finding a teacher, overcoming stage fright, dress code, and performing at different occasions.

The only requirement you need is your voice and, ideally, two tape recorders: one to play the pre-recorded tape that accompanies this course and the other to record your singing.

Teach Yourself Singing will inform and guide you towards a better understanding of your voice and your potential. The path to progress is viewed from two standpoints: developing an instrument and developing the skills of the instrumentalist.

Be realistic about your goals. Don't be held back by limited expectations, but remember that although you can be taught to make the best of your voice, you cannot develop it beyond the limits of its capabilities.

Lesson plans are flexible, so add exercises from throughout the book, if you feel that they will help to enhance your particular performance. All the methods and exercises are fully explained so you understand the reason and purpose for each procedure. Some of the advice is intended to help sort out specific problems, so dip into the book to answer any queries you may have.

It is not essential to be able to read music before you start the course, because the tape will play everything you need to hear, just as a tape of spoken French might accompany a French course. However, if you are able to read music, it is possible to use this book without the cassette, but I would strongly recommend that you purchase the cassette to make the best of the course. You will find the full piano accompaniment to the songs printed at the end of each lesson plan, as played on the cassette.

As you become familiar with handling pieces of music, you will notice that many of the same terms and signs crop up time after time. Written music is included, so that you can quickly become fluent in the language of music, and a glossary is provided at the end of the book to help you understand the meaning of each sign and term.

Part One

BEFORE YOU SING

1

YOUR BODY, YOUR INSTRUMENT

You are the instrument, as far as singing is concerned, so even though you haven't had to buy an expensive piece of equipment in order to make music, don't assume that your body will look after itself. An exhausted or sick singer can't give a tremendous performance; fitness is a major consideration. Physical and vocal exercise, coupled with mental agility, provide a foundation for the work to come. It is also important to consider such things as food which may affect the sound you make. Citrus fruit, milky drinks, alcohol, chocolate, fatty meals, anything that is either difficult to digest, or has an astringent or clogging affect on the natural mucus in the throat, will affect your voice. You should try not to sing when you have a sore throat as this will only aggravate the inflamed tissue. When the weather is cold or windy protect your throat and mouth by covering them with a scarf. When you sing, make sure that you really are 'warmed up' and that means your whole body and not just the throat area.

If your voice refuses to work in one area where it has worked well before, perhaps you are over-using this register without proper preparation. Good voice production relies upon effective muscle response and those muscles must be properly and regularly exercised.

If you were learning to play the piano, you wouldn't expect to make progress without practice. It is just the same when you learn to sing. You have to be patient and prepared to invest a little of your time each day. Listen to your voice and hear what it is trying to tell you.

The voice reflects our innermost feelings, and is also an accurate barometer of our health. Take care of your voice; you can't go out and buy another one.

—— How The Voice Works ——

The voice relies upon the successful co-operation between the larynx or 'voice-box', and those muscles by which the larynx is suspended. When we speak the muscles stretch or ease the tension on the vocal chords and control their rate of vibration, altering the pitch of the voice. Air passes over the vocal chords and becomes the bearer of sound.

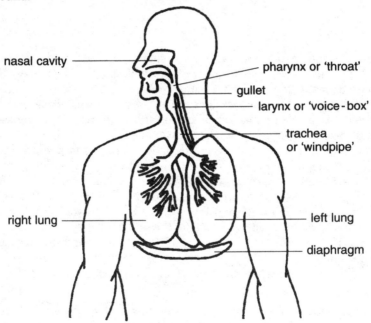

nasal cavity

pharynx or 'throat'

gullet

larynx or 'voice-box'

trachea or 'windpipe'

right lung

left lung

diaphragm

Figure 1   The organ of breathing

When you take a breath, the rib-cage expands, the diaphragm lowers and flattens out, allowing the lungs to expand and fill with air.

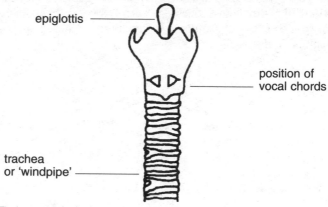

Figure 2　The larynx or 'voice-box'

Like any other instrument, the body has resonators which amplify the colour and sound. However, unlike many other instruments, some of the body's resonaters are able to change shape. Resonators occur in body space where the sound of the voice, and vibrations set up by that sound, are able to reach. Vocal resonators include chest spaces, throat spaces, the mouth, the skull and the nasal passages which include three sinus passages.

The *vocal chords* are two folds of tissue stretched out across the very top of the trachea, or windpipe, in a cavity called the larynx (see figure 3). During normal breathing they lie at rest and air passes freely between them. The space between the vocal chords is called the *glottis*.

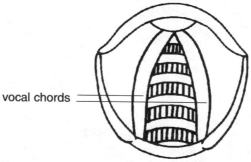

Figure 3　The trachea showing the glottis open

Muscles in the neck and larynx are able to draw the chords together so that they are almost touching. These movements can be controlled, allowing a variety of sounds to be produced including speech, singing, coughing and sneezing.

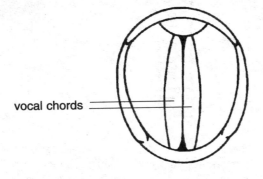

Figure 4   The trachea showing the glottis closed

2
-PREPARING YOUR BODY-

————————— **Relaxation** —————————

It might seem a contradiction in terms to consider relaxation right at the beginning of an energetic course like this rather than at the end, but tension affects voice production and you must be in a poised and receptive state when you begin to sing.

Here are some physical exercises which will make you aware of any sneaky tensions lurking in your body. They will take only a few minutes at the beginning of each lesson, but their benefits will be well worth the effort. As well as easing physical tension, they will help you to focus your thoughts and ensure that your posture is correct before you begin.

Relaxation exercise 1

- Keeping your legs straight, gently bend forwards, allowing your arms and upper torso to lean towards the floor.
- Relax. Let your arms dangle loosely for a slow count of five, then swing them back and forth through your legs, up and through, five times, very gently. Every part of you from the waist up should now be relaxed.
- Carefully straighten until you are standing.
- Bring your arms up slowly and stretch towards the ceiling. Feel

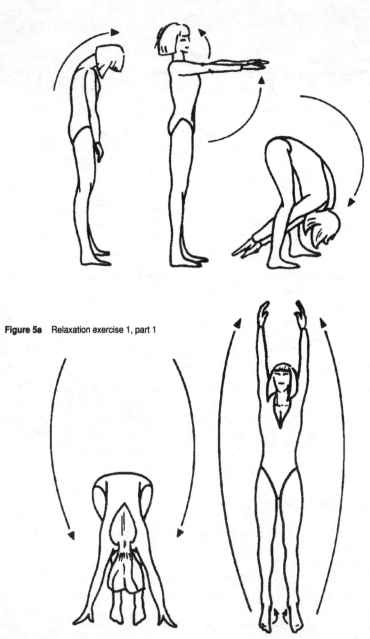

Figure 5a Relaxation exercise 1, part 1

Figure 5b Relaxation exercise 1, part 2

the stretch go right through your body, from your toes to your fingertips.

- Hold the stretch for the moment, then relax into a well-balanced standing position with your feet slightly apart, and bring your arms slowly down to the sides of your body.
- Repeat this manoeuvre three times.

Relaxation exercise 2

- Are your shoulders relaxed? Keeping your head level and your neck still, bring your left shoulder forward, lift it and roll it back, allowing it to settle in the most comfortable position for you.
- Repeat this action three times and then repeat the manoeuvre with the right shoulder.
- Complete the exercise by using both shoulders at once.
- Repeat the whole procedure three times.

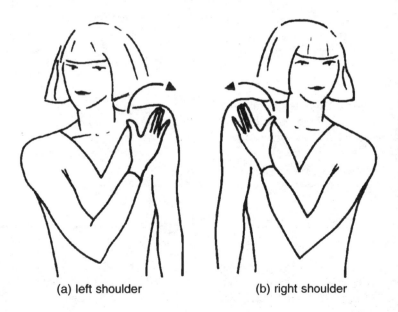

(a) left shoulder   (b) right shoulder

Figure 6   Relaxation exercise 2, part 1

Relaxation exercise 3

Hands can show more tension clearly than almost any other part of the body and you want soft expressive hands that will be unobtrusive in repose but will be ready to make a graceful gesture, if required, so try this clench and release exercise.

- Draw your left hand into a tight ball and hold for a slow count of five, then relax.
- Perform this exercise five times, then repeat with the right hand.
- Finally, exercise both hands together, five times.

These exercises are all useful at the beginning of a lesson, but at the end of a long, hard day, you could use the clench and release exercise to relax your whole body. You will need to lie down and clench and release the muscles in each area of the body separately. Finally, tighten all the muscles in your body and hold for a slow count of five. When you relax, you will experience a most extraordinary floating sensation.

Posture

The torso is the power-house of the voice and like the body of any other instrument must not be crumpled. The stomach should be firm, the rib-cage lifted and extended, and the shoulders wide, rather than rounded or thrust back.

To check whether your rib-cage is extending, put your hands around your torso, with your thumbs at your back and with the finger tips of each hand touching at the front of your body. Now take a breath in. Your fingertips should move apart and there should be no movement in your shoulders. Only use this exercise to experience the sensation of extending the rib-cage. Once you are familiar with the correct position, your muscles will be able to accomplish the task and you will need your breath to sing.

Figure 8   Extending the ribcage

Keep your head level and chin parallel with the floor and be conscious of the signals you deliver with your body position. If you hold your shoulders, upper arms and elbows too far back you will appear arrogant or even aggressive. But bring your shoulders forward and you will seem apologetic. Take a few moments to review your position. Relax your shoulders and hands, tuck in your bottom, draw in your stomach. Be sure you are standing in a well-balanced way, with your weight evenly distributed on the balls of your feet, one foot slightly in front of the other, and your knees flexed rather than locked.

Don't appear to be set like cement: a living, breathing person moves a little even when they are standing still.

Your performance space is all around you as far as you can reach upwards and outwards; aim to inhabit it spiritually if not physically. Don't strike a pose – your appearance should be as natural as possible, even though you will be on a higher plane of awareness than usual. Feel poised, confident and happy.

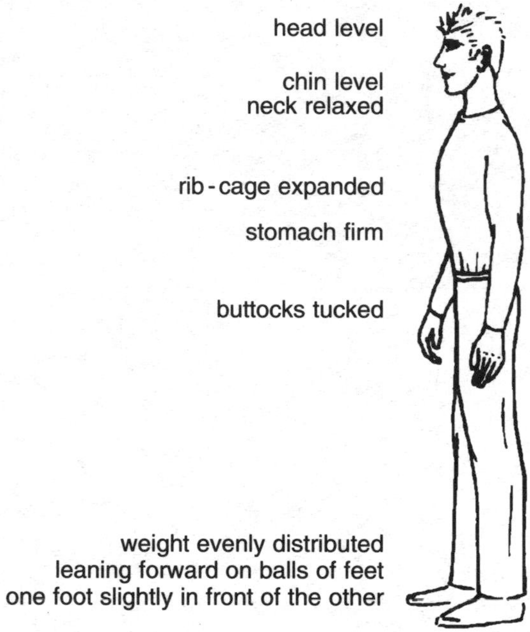

head level

chin level
neck relaxed

rib - cage expanded

stomach firm

buttocks tucked

weight evenly distributed
leaning forward on balls of feet
one foot slightly in front of the other

Figure 9 Standing position with weight evenly distributed

Breathing

'Can you help me with my breathing?' This is a question with which most singing teachers are familiar. Why should breathing, an involuntary action, suddenly pose a problem for a singer?

The whole point is that far from taking it for granted, the singer has to *think* about breathing; when to do it, how to extend the breath, how to eke out or plan the breath, how to breath quietly, how to use the actual fact of taking a breath to create a dramatic point, how to direct the flow of air to move swiftly, slowly, or not at all. The song may require you to take a breath before you feel the need or to wait longer than is comfortable before you breathe.

Singing is an extremely energetic activity, and the breaths you take in have more in common with those needed to fulfil the physical demands of sport, rather than the lethargic tiny and frequent breaths of general life. The singer may appear poised and calm, with no outward show of effort or the sound of noisy breathing, but, if the song requires it, he or she could be breathing as energetically, swiftly and efficiently as when engaged in sport. This section will help you to learn to breath effectively, maximising the use of air you take in.

Some basic points to remember

1 You must feel mentally poised and ready for action.
2 Your body must be prepared to make to make some really energetic actions internally, whilst you maintain a calm exterior.
3 Try not to think of breathing as a one-dimensional action involving only the front of your body, but imagine the lungs as a tyre that goes right around the upper body. The back and sides of the upper body expand when the lungs are filled, not just the chest.
4 Remember that your shoulders should play no part in your breathing and neither should your stomach. Don't allow you shoulders to rise, or your stomach to bulge when you breath in.
5 Correct breathing for the singer is controlled by the mid-section of the body. High, tense breathing is of no use.
6 Be careful not to 'over-breathe'. Over-filling the lungs with air will only make you feel uncomfortable and lead to upper body tension. This causes the air to gush and be wasted as soon as you make the first sound.
7 The amount of air required to appreciate the scent of a beautiful flower, taken in silently through the mouth, should be adequate for your needs.
8 Don't confuse big breaths with energetic breaths.
   Big breaths, see point 6, are *wrong*.
   Energetic breaths, see point 2 are *correct*.
9 When you are ready to sing, try not to draw in a sluggish, long,

'planned' breath. Let your breathing respond spontaneously to the music and to the words you are to sing.

10 Breathe so that the musical line and the sense of the words you sing remain whole.

11 Never take a breath 'just to be on the safe side'.

12 Don't waste your breath. Two of the main culprits of this are:

　i Unconsciously putting in a extra 'h' between notes to articulate a change of pitch. This is not the correct way to do this and apart from wasting your breath, it will make your pronunciation of the words sound unnatural.

　ii Get straight on to the first note, don't unconsciously sigh out air before you begin to sing.

13 Less air is needed to create a pure, focused sound, rather than a breathy or husky note.

14 Allow flexibility in your breathing plan, as this may change as you become more familiar with the song. The speed at which you sing will also affect your breathing.

15 Check that you are allowing the lungs to do their work. To develop good breath support, it may help you to think of squeezing a tube of toothpaste from the bottom to get the last squirt of paste. Use your stomach muscles for support and use all your breath.

16 Do not round your shoulders and become tense as you use up your breath, as this will squeeze and restrict your lungs.

17 Read the section on posture (see page 8) before you attempt any of the breathing exercises.

REMEMBER...

When you make a pause, or take a breath, the music continues. Don't sing a phrase, then collapse mentally and physically before you sing the next phrase. This breaks the musical line and makes very heavy weather out of singing.

Singing to the very end of the breath in a long phrase does cause some discomfort. When you first start singing, you may breathe as soon as you feel uncomfortable, but singers train, as do athletes, on a progressive programme of activities to increase their stamina. Athletes become accustomed to 'the burn' and learn to work through it. The singer feels the discomfort of the extra effort to begin with, but once accustomed to the sensation, is able to banish it from their thoughts. Nothing should come between you and your music making.

And finally ...

Anything that appears tense, forced, strained or unnatural cannot be right. Singing is a musical extension of your personality; an amplification in sound and drama, perhaps, but still, unmistakably, you.

Breathing exercise 1

Read through this exercise, then close your eyes if it helps you to concentrate.

- Correct your posture than draw in a steady breath through your nose to a slow count of three.
- Wait for a count of three, don't hold the breath at the back of the throat; think of the breath as being suspended, rather than held.
- Allow the breath to flow out in a steady stream through pursed lips. It will take longer to exhale in a controlled manner; a count of five would be about right. Listen to the soft, blowing breath and keep it even. Wait for a slow count of three.
- Repeat the exercise until you feel calm and in control.

Developments of breathing exercise 1

- The noise you use as you breathe out can be varied, for example, 'S', 'Z', rolled 'R', 'V', humming, etc.
- The number counts can be extended as your confidence and capacity grow, but remember the aim of the exercise is to develop breath control not to break any records, so hold your breath for as long as you feel comfortable.
- You could use this controlled breathing strategy in your everyday life. For instance, as you walk down the road, match your paces to your counting.

Breathing exercise 2

- Lie down on a flat surface.
- Slowly raise your right leg to an angle of ninety degrees to the

body, or as close as you can manage.

- Breathe steadily as you hold the position, to a count of three, then lower the leg gently to the floor.
- Repeat with your left leg.
- Finally, repeat the exercise raising both legs at the same time. Try not to bend your legs. You will feel a strong pull on your abdomen. This will help to tighten up muscles which, if allowed to grow slack, will inhibit the abdominal support that is required for proper breathing.
- Repeat the whole exercise five times.

Breathing exercise 3

- Imagine that you are entering a room. You see a letter addressed to you on the table.
- You pick the letter up and begin to read.
- Startled, or just pleasantly surprised, you exclaim, 'Ah'. The swift and spontaneous breath you took before you exclaimed is right for most of your singing.

Breathing exercise 4

- Draw in a deep silent breath, then let it out, either through the nose or the mouth.
- Do not inhale again, but sharply force out the residual air in your lungs – '*Puh*'! You will hear another involuntary sound as air is drawn back spontaneously into the lungs – '*Uh*'. The instant recovery of some of the exhaled breath is caused by the relaxation of the breathing muscles.
- Repeat the '*Puh-uh*' exercise several times, but be careful not to hyperventilate. You will feel faint if you overdo this exercise.

Become accustomed to the totally tension-free feel of that involuntary recovery breath, 'Uh'. That is exactly how 'open' you should feel when you take a snatched breath in singing.

That lack of tension ensures that what might seem to you to be a very quick, even shallow, breath is actually filling your lungs far more than you imagined.

This is a particularly useful exercise to avoid the ugly sound known as 'Glottal Stop', which occurs when the singer slams into the breath with the result that a noise similar to throat clearing immediately precedes a vowel sound.

Breathing exercise 5

Unless you want to make a dramatic point with a noisy intake of breath, breathing while singing should be silent. Vocalised, noisy breath occurs when the vocal chords are brought into play, rather than allowing the air to pass freely through the glottis. As soon as the chords begin to close, sound is created.

- Listen now as you sigh noisily, then gasp aloud.
- Next, imagine yourself breathing as softly as you can, as if you were hiding from someone. It is possible to breathe silently, the secret is to rid yourself of all tension in the throat. think of the airways as being wide and free, rather than narrow and constricted.

Breathing exercise 6

- Breathe out.
- Bend forwards comfortably as far as you can. Put your hand over the soft part of your back between your rib-cage and your pelvis and breathe in.
- You should feel the inner expansion here, as your lungs fill with air.

Make sure that when you breathe you are aware that this area will fill and expand with air in just the same way that you expect the front and sides of your body to expand.

Breathing exercise 7

- Breathe in deeply and steadily through your nose.
- Exhale the same amount of air gently through your mouth.
- Now try to sing a few notes of a familiar tune.
- You may be surprised to discover just how much you can sing, having 'breathed out', using the residual air in the lungs. This exercise is a great confidence- booster.

Always remember that until you are familiar with a song and accustomed to the physical demands the performance makes on your body, your breathing plan will develop, to some degree, by trial and error. This is quite natural and does not mean that you have any particular breathing problems.

- Plan where you are going to breathe in keeping with the musical line and sense the words.
- Sing the phrases then the song as many times as you need to experience and to remember the flow of breath required.
- Make necessary adjustments to your breath flow as you become more familiar with the song.

3

—— PRONUNCIATION ——

Clear speech is the pre-requisite of intelligible singing. It is important to remember that an actor seldom faces much competition when he begins his soliloquy. A singer, on the other hand, usually has some accompaniment to distract the audience, so his delivery must not only be informed and authoritative, but absolutely intelligible. Singing in a foreign language is no excuse for poor diction. The words of a piece should be understood, respected and enjoyed.

In order to communicate effectively, you must deliver your message clearly. In your mind you have an image of what you want to convey and you should use all your physical skills to transform that image into reality.

As a singer you aim for clarity of mood, of musical realisation, and of pronunciation. The listeners should be left in no doubt as to your intentions. They must receive an accurate impression, unimpeded by anything that lies within your power to influence. An artistic creation exists to be shared and nothing should be allowed to obstruct that process.

If you were to sing approximately the right notes with approximately the correct time values, you fall short in your duty to act as the medium through which the composer's musical message is transmitted. In the same way, if you sing beautifully, yet incoherently, you withhold the possibility of maximum pleasure, both for yourself and your audience, because the words, which may have inspired the composition in the first place, will be lost.

The use of vowel sounds and consonants

We recognise five main *vowel* sounds, 'a, e, i, o, u', but in fact there are many others, since a vowel is any speech or sung sound made by allowing the voiced breath to pass in a continuous stream through the throat and open mouth. This definition shows that sound travels best on vowels, so they should be both clear and distinctive, one from another.

Diphthongs occur when one vowel takes on the sound of two as its initial sound slides into another. This can sound ugly in song and unless called for by a specific style of music, the vowel slide of the diphthong is kept as close to the end of the sung note as possible.

A *consonant* is any speech or sung sound that is produced by obstructing the flow of voiced breath in any one of a number of ways. The singer aims for that obstruction or interruption to be split-second.

If you are using amplification, singing 'on consonants' is possible, even desirable, when invoking certain moods. If on the other hand, your performance depends upon projecting the voice effectively and without artificial aids, you must extend your vowel sounds and compact your consonants. A clear delivery of consonants depends upon nimble movements by the tongue and lips and upon effective interaction between breath, lips, tongue, teeth and soft and hard palate.

Some consonants have the effect of 'bringing the voice forward'. You may be familiar with the sensation of your voice 'going back' in your throat, so that it almost feels as if the throat is coated with a layer of sound. This type of production sounds weak and tires the voice quickly.

Many of the vocal exercises you will find in the book use a 'lip' consonant, such as 'm', 'p', 'l' to help you think and propel the vowel sound forward.

Tips to remember before doing the exercises

- Don't be tempted to linger over the 'm', or leave a gap between 'm', and your vowel. 'M' is one of the 'voiced' consonants and so must be in tune with the note you sing on the vowel sound.

- Use the consonant as a springboard that launches you onto the vowel sound. See how quickly you can move from 'm' to the vowel.

- Say the sounds clearly and be careful not to overmouth. Your intention is to look as natural as possible and to achieve a similar, balanced quality of sound throughout the exercise.

- Open your mouth, but not too wide; allow the jaw to drop open gently and without tension; keep your tongue relaxed and out of the way. The tongue should not become rigid as it is an essential element in the construction of vowel sounds and will move about to some degree, but it should generally be kept low in the mouth. The tip, especially, should not tense and curl upwards. The soft palate should be arched in the 'yawning' position, again without tension.

- To improve your delivery of consonants, it will help to exercise your tongue and lips. In many cases, the tip of the tongue is the cause of the problem.

  Instead of trying to use the whole length of the tongue to form the consonant 'l', feel the difference when you mobilise just the tip. Bring the tongue forward so that you flick the tip on your hard palate just behind your top teeth. Now you should be able to repeat the 'l' consonant quite easily.

Vocal Exercises

1 Prefix two vowel sounds with the consonant 'm'. Pronounce the vowels in the Italian manner – that is, don't say, 'layee', rather than plain 'le', or 'la-uh' instead of 'la': 'e' as the 'a' in 'gate'; 'a' as in 'father', 'Le,le, la'.

Join the vowel sounds together in an arc of sound, flicking the tongue briskly to make the 'l' as unintrusive as possible. The flow of breath remains constant throughout this spoken exercise.

Italian vowel sounds are commonly used in singing exercises. If more than one vowel sound is required, more than one vowel is used. In other words, the placement of each vowel sound is planned, rather than haphazard.

2 Practice this exercise before you meet it in the vocal exercise section. It uses five Italian vowel sounds, 'a, e, i, o, u', prefixed by the lip consonant, 'm', 'ma, me, mi, mo, mu'.

Ma – 'a' as in father

Me – 'e' as the 'a' in gate

Mi – 'i' as in machine

Mo – 'o' as in the 'oo' in door

Mu – 'u' as in the 'oo' in cool

The pronunciation is different to the English pronunciation of the same vowels and there should be no diphthongs.

N.B. To produce the 'm' sound, the lips come together smartly and spring apart, allowing the vowel sounds to flow and be projected forward with the minimum interruption. Once again, the flow of breath remains constant throughout the exercise and the 'm' must be exactly in tune with the vowel sound.

– Why you should do vocal exercises –

You want to make the most of your voice. You want to hear an even tone produced from the top to the bottom of your range. You want to develop a technique that can cope equally well with high notes, low notes and all the notes in between, whether you sing slowly or rapidly. You will achieve these aims with regular exercise.

Like athletes, singers work themselves up gradually to full power using exercises called scales. Scales are an ascending or descending sequence of notes which exercise all those muscles you will be using when you sing your songs. Exercises on a single note are also useful, because they give you an opportunity to listen to the sound you make, its quality and its pitch accuracy. Leaps from one note to another, higher or lower in pitch, and arpeggios, where the notes are not so close together as scales, but still the voice must rise and fall maintaining an even tone quality, will all help your muscles to become stronger, more flexible and accustomed to their new task.

Exercises help you to make the vital transition from the staccato, or short and detached patterns of speech, to the sustained sound of song. They will help you to break free from the polite, moderate volume of speech and allow you to experience a far wider range of dynamics.

— Changing emotions in your songs —

The narrow band of pitch variation used in speech will be expanded and your ability to weave ever more intricate strands of notes, in progressively longer and more complex patterns, will be developed. You are already using some degree of tone colour and expression in speech. How many times have you said 'You sound happy today .. or sad ... or angry'? All human emotions are reflected in the voice.

The singer serves two masters, music and poetry, so once you are familiar with the vocal exercises, colour the sound you make with different emotions. You could try big mood swings to start with; happy, sad, then draw in the contrast until you are able to express the subtle change between say, exuberance and joy, or grief and regret.

You don't want to make just any sound, you want to make the best sound possible. A sound you feel comfortable with. A sound that is round, full and promising, not flat, thin and irritating. Clear and steady vowel sounds and, to start with, free from regional variation. The voice can be trained in time to do different things but if you try to be too ambitious too soon, disaster will follow. Once you have brought the voice up to its peak and learned how to use it, accents, tone, colour, dynamics will only be restricted by your imagination. Remember though, if you don't provide fuel for your imagination, it's development will be stunted and the possibilities for you will be restricted.

The Tongue

If you tend to have lazy speech patterns, they will be exposed when you sing. You have probably never considered the mobility of your tongue before, but now you are going to spend some time working on it, as well as considering whether you are maximising the interaction between your tongue, teeth and lips. Exercising helps you to become more aware of how flexible or not you are. Set aside about 20 minutes at least twice a week to do these exercises.

Tongue exercises

● Try touching the tip of your nose with your tongue... Easier for some than for others!

- Stick your tongue out as far as you can, then out to each side in turn, down to your chin up to your nose. Repeat this three times.

- Repeat the word 'letter' several times.
- Make the repititions faster and faster.
- Open your mouth so that the sound resonates clearly.

- There are various tongue twisters you can use to identify problem areas. Here are a few to wrap your tongue around:

> Red leather, yellow leather
> Selfish shellfish
> Fresh flat fish
> Six shrunken skirts
> Sharp shrews sweet shop
> Ten pin thin tin trunks
> Red lorry, yellow lorry

If you find the 'r' consonant nearly impossible to execute, growl low down in your throat: 'grrrh!'. The tongue, even if it will not roll or vibrate with the passage of air you force over it, will move quite firmly from curled up, to flat as you expel the air to make the 'h' sound. Now take the 'g' away, 'rrrh!' If you trim off the superfluous air blast, which you have used to make the 'h' sound, you will be left with enough tongue movement to allow you to produce a satisfactory 'r'.

Here is some more work for your tongue which you do with your mouth closed.

- Drop your jaw to allow more space within the mouth cavity, whilst keeping your mouth closed. Now move your tongue rapidly from side to side; then from top to bottom (for this last, you use just the tip). [You may find this exercise makes you want to yawn.] Just before you leave this closed mouth, dropped jaw position, explore the insides of your mouth – you will discover quite a cavern. The ideal resonator in fact.

- Now reduce the space inside your closed mouth dramatically by relaxing your jaw. explore again. This time you will feel an extremely restricted space with your tongue, from which you cannot reasonably expect resonant, ringing sounds to emerge.

The Lips

Mobile lips are both an important and attractive asset. Without taking this to ridiculous lengths, consider most of the fascinating people you know – I'm sure none of them is 'tight-lipped'. The mouth is one of your most expressive features, and the lips are crucial to word formation.

Lip exercises

Here are some exercises which I advise you to perform either under cover of darkness, or in a securely locked room! In any case, make them a vital part of your studies. Just a few minutes, once or twice a week, will help to improve the mobility of your lips.

● Bring your mouth forward, lips together and puckered up tightly as if about to deliver a kiss.
Open and close just the tightened lips without relaxing the mouth, like a goldfish.
Repeat several times.

● With mouth closed, face bright and smiling, extend the smile as far as you can, stretching your lips out to the side.
Quickly bring your lips together in the goldfish pout and scowl ...
Smile, scowl, smile, scowl, smile, scowl, etc.

● Close your mouth, completely relax your lips, puff them out softly and blow through them.
If they are relaxed enough they should vibrate really well.

● Using a low pitch and with your mouth barely open and lips relaxed, hum. You should be able to feel your lips tingle.

● Make your face as small as possible, by imagining that you are drawing every part of your face into one central point. Hold for a count of three.
Now make your face as large as possible, like an inflated balloon. Puff out your checks. Open your eyes wide. Hold for a count of three, then repeat the exercise three times.

● Use an exaggerated chewing motion for one minute.

● Pretend your mouth is a rubber band.
Stretch it wide in every imaginable direction.

Conclusion

Identify possible problems of pronunciation in the text of songs before you begin to sing.

Always read through the words first. Not only will this help you to spot the potential difficulties in pronunciation, it will also allow you to absorb the meaning, mood and 'pace' of a piece. For instance, where do the inflections occur, where do you feel the urge to push on, and where to linger? It will not always be possible to transfer your interpretation direct and intact from text to song, but you should gain a much clearer impression of what you want to do, when you **are** ready to combine the two.

When you listen to yourself sing, learn to be discriminating by listening to as many singers as possible and to as much good music as you can, so that your appreciation of what is good and what is not so good, becomes progressively more refined.

Remember to open your mouth! Not as silly as it sounds, for a small aperture will only allow a small sound to emerge and you want a beautiful note. So think of a cavern shape rather than a fried egg shape. Don't overdo it, or you'll look ridiculous and feel uncomfortable. Use a mirror, whenever possible, to check your appearance.

Release your breath in a steady stream. Don't allow it to stop and start, or run slow and then blast. Imagine a bow stroke on a violin, rather than the percussive effect you might expect from a piano.

Keep the tone even. If the sound is 'weedy' mentally remove the walls and ceiling of your room. You are now singing in a theatre and your audience is waiting. Don't force the sound. Think 'pure and purposeful'. Direct your voice forward with energy, never force. Focus the sound into a beam of light. No tightening or tension must shadow that beam as it travels through your mouth. Is the sound cold and meaningless? Even an exercise should have appeal, both to the listener and to you. There should be thought behind the sound.

Keep in tune. To begin with, play the note or the tape each time and listen carefully to make sure you match its pitch exactly. Singing is as much about developing your listening skills, as it is about developing the vocal instrument.

When you use a single note exercise that requires you to sing several different vowel sounds on that one note, are you achieving an even and similar tone each time, or does one vowel sound have a different quality to the rest?

Are you straight onto the note each time you sing, or swooping up to it and having to make an adjustment? Land effortlessly, right on the note and be satisfied with nothing less. Approximations will not do.

The voice is as much an instrument as any other and it is quite right that you should want to achieve the same level of expertise as your fellow musicians, but don't try to sing through all the exercises at once as this will defeat their object.

Be sensitive about your developing skills as you work through the course and be ready to adjust your daily programme as required. In other words, you are both student and teacher.

When you feel that your exercise programme is working really well, don't be afraid to slip in something completely new.

Always keep the programme flexible, responsive and relevant to the songs you are studying.

In the moment before you make a sound, appreciate silence. Concentrate on that silence now while you breathe deeply.

4
CONFIDENT PROJECTION

Your problem is that you are unable to sing above a whisper. Your speaking voice may not draw attention to itself, being the usual volume of most people's voices. It rises in pitch in response to questions or to express surprise and drops in pitch to murmur confidentially or express sympathy. It remains at a polite volume and does not single you out for special attention. On the other hand, your singing voice is feeble when you feel it should have a similar capacity for communicating in song. Pitch variations, as along as they remain within fairly narrow boundaries to start with, shouldn't be a problem and neither should expression. The remaining points to consider are volume, control and the fact that by singing, you **are** drawing attention to yourself.

Volume

We are so used to operating vocally at a polite level for speech, that it takes some experimentation and courage to break away from that restraint. You are aiming to deliver an accurate and appealing musical message, but aren't used to raising your voice to make pleasant sounds for any length of time. Most warm and charming speech sounds are uttered at a moderate volume. Singing takes you beyond that threshold.

The sound you will make when you sing is more penetrating and is sustained over a long period of time. Therefore it must be evaluated and moulded with far more care than is necessary for speech. Think for a moment before you utter a sound. Have you never raised your voice in anger, never called out to attract attention, never laughed uncontrollably, never raised your voice in the whole of your life ...?

The one certainty is that you **can** raise your voice. Accept that fact and you are already on your way to producing a bigger sound.

Control

Just as breathing can pose an unnecessary problem for some people when it ceases to be an involuntary action and becomes instead a considered and planned action, so can the simple act of raising the volume of your voice in a considered and planned way. All your previous outbursts of yelling and guffawing may have been spontaneous, but now you are required to raise the volume of your voice and monitor its quality while you do so.

To begin with you may not like what you hear but don't let that put you off. Only by trial and error will you come to recognise the good sounds from the bad.

Drawing attention to yourself

At first you may be content to practise in solitude, but singing is all about giving, sharing and joining in. Eventually you will want to sing with people and to people. At some stage, by the very act of singing, you will draw attention to yourself, but is that such a bad thing? When you have something good to offer, why not share it?

Part Two

STARTING TO SING

5

SUGGESTED DAILY PROGRAMME

Jerome Hines to Luciano Pavarotti. 'Do you still do scales?'

Maestro Pavarotti, 'Of course, every day.'

Muscles need to be exercised and a discriminating ear needs the opportunity to develop. Start with ten to fifteen minutes of exercise once or preferably twice a day. Your body's physical characteristics and stamina, combined with the degree of your eagerness to learn, will determine how this practice time increases. Shorter bursts of concentrated effort are more effective than tedious marathons.

Think of yourself as a member of an orchestra, tuning up. You are listening carefully to your instrument and learning a great deal about your general health and state of mind as you do so. You are setting an appropriate volume, quite a way above the level of polite speech, but still controlled and attractive. Your body and mind are fully committed to the act of music-making.

Relaxation/Posture

Are you standing well and without tension. Are your shoulders, or hands tense? Make any necessary adjustments. Use the relaxation exercises on pages 5–8 if you need them.

Breathing

Close your eyes and take a few deep breaths in through the nose, out through the mouth, while you prepare yourself mentally. You could practise some of the breathing exercises shown on pages 13–16 to help with your preparation.

Exercises

Exercise 1

ma ..   me ..   mi ..   mo ..   mu ..

You are making the transition from spoken to sung sound. You are alert and listening carefully. You retain a sense of inner tranquillity.

Work within a three note range either side of your starting note, 'Ma, me, mi, mo, mu'. You are listening for evenness of tone, volume and pitch. The notes should all be on one 'bow stroke'. The sound is very warm, charming and steady.

Continue with the exercise identifying those sounds which you enjoy most. Use those good sounds as a model for the rest.

When you are satisfied, see if the voice will 'run' for you, moving easily and evenly from one note to the next.

Exercise 2

ma .. me .. mi .. mo ..   mu——

Working within a small range, don't put any pressure on the voice or try to make an 'important' sound. Don't waste breath, focus is what you are after. If you do put pressure on, or try to force the sound in any way, your voice will be unwieldy and will not run evenly up and down this short exercise, 'Ma, me, mi, mo, mu'.

Exercise 3

mu ——————————————————
u ——————————————————

Repeat the last vowel sound used in the previous exercise, ensuring that, without over-mouthing, you make a really pure 'oo' sound, rather than a lazy sound that tends towards 'uh'.

 Exercise 4

ma .. me .. mi .. mo .. mu ——————————
ma .. me .. mi .. mo .. mu ——————————

Put a repeat into Exercise 2. Do not take a breath in the middle, one breath is enough for the whole exercise. Learn not to waste your breath, but allow the flow to be sufficient to create a full, pure sound.

 Exercise 5

(a) ah .... eh .... oh .... ee .... ah
(b) :‖

Listen for even and easy vocal production. Don't 'dig in' to the lower notes. The whole exercise should be clear and fluid, 'Ah, eh, oh, ee, ah'.

 Exercise 6

now   sing   for   jo -   -   -   -   -   y

You want to achieve an evenness of tone quality and volume from top to bottom of this exercise and also a high degree of musical accuracy; 'Now sing for joy'.

Exercise 7

'Joy', unaccompanied and accompanied. Exercising from the top of the exercise with control and clarity.

Exercise 8

Back to 'Ma, me, mi, mo, mu', this time a longer exercise requiring a high degree of accuracy, as well as excellent vocal and breath control.

Exercise 9

Don't forget to work on the notes of your lower range. Keep them natural, bright and well balanced with those of your higher register.

Use your final note of the previous exercise as a starting point for 'Grey Skies'.

There are two more exercises that will help you balance the voice between higher and lower notes. These can be found in lesson plan 4 'Ah no'.

All these exercises should be practised both accompanied and unaccompanied. Record your singing whenever possible and don't be too harsh on yourself! 'Warming up' is all about achieving the best possible sound, but your sound will improve, given time and attention. It will also be better on some days than others, because your voice is a living, breathing instrument.

By the end of the exercise session, your throat should not feel tired or tense. If it does, you have done too much too soon, or have sung out too loud, or have found some other way of putting too much pressure on your voice. You may have even disturbed the site of an infection.

Your voice should feel easy and the sound should be full, rather than edgy, harsh or breathy. Use the exercises contained within the following seven lesson plans to vary your approach and to address specific areas. If you remember that your voice will not always respond as you want it to, or expect it to, you will not become bogged down with one particular exercise or locked into one tedious routine. Spend just a few attentive minutes on each exercise and be prepared to have a flexible approach.

—— Summary of daily programme ——

- Relaxation/Posture.
- Breathing.
- Vocal exercises which may be drawn from the following:
  1 'Ma, me, mi, mo, mu' – on a single note.
  2 'Ma, me, mi, mo, mu' – five note exercise.
  3 'Oo.'
  4 'Ma, me, mi, mo, mu – five-note exercise with a repeat.
  5 'Ah, eh, oh, ee, ah.'
  6 'Now sing for joy.'
  7 'Joy.'
  8 'Ma, me, mi, mo, mu – a longer scale.'
  9 'Grey skies.'

You will become the best judge of what suits your particular needs and will be able to compose some additional exercises.

If you go on to a teacher, you will find that they have their own unique approach. One of the richest sources of exercise material will come from songs you sing. If a particular part troubles you, take it out and use it as an exercise, break it down into its component parts and try to analyse the problem. If you simply sing through a song allowing a particular section to remain a trouble spot, you will not be improving your technique and you are never going to be satisfied with your singing.

The following lesson plans are structured to revolve around a song, each practising particular skills. A list of objectives is found at the beginning of the lesson plan to show the skills involved. Vocal exercises are included in each lesson plan to prepare and lead the student up to a confident public performance.

6
LESSON PLAN 1
'Morning has Broken'

OBJECTIVES

To produce a clear and focused tone.
To keep the tone even, flowing and well-balanced.
To sing through to the end of a musical phrase.
To deliver the words of the song in a natural and convincing manner.

Silently read through the words. Places to breathe are marked with a tick ✓.

Marks indicating optional breaths appear in brackets (✓).

Where you breathe is also decided by the speed at which you decide to sing each song. However many breaths you take, they must be in an appropriate place, so that the sense of the words and the musical line remain whole.

Morning has broken (✓) like the first morning, ✓
Blackbird has spoken (✓) like the first bird. ✓
Praise for the singing, ✓ praise for the morning, ✓
Praise for the springing (✓) fresh from the word. ✓

Sweet the rain's new fall, ✓ sunlit from heaven, ✓
Like the first dew-fall (✓) on the first grass. ✓
Praise for the sweetness (✓) of the wet garden, ✓
Sprung in completeness (✓) where His feet pass.

> Mine is the sunlight, ✓ mine is the morning, ✓
> Born of the one light (✓) Eden saw play. ✓
> Praise with elation, ✓ praise every morning, ✓
> God's recreation ✓ of the new day. ✓

You may think that there are a lot of ticks, but it is far better to take a breath provided it does not spoil the musical line or the sense of the words, rather than to allow the tone to dwindle or collapse altogether. As you become more confident and accustomed to singing, you will find that your capacity for extending the vocal line increases.

The mood suggested by both the words and style of music is sincerity and simplicity. Whether or not the sentiments are your own, the actor in you comes to the fore. The words are beautiful, so make them count. Enjoy and think about them now as you read the poem out loud.

You will have found that some words require more emphasis than others, or you may have wanted to linger over a certain phrase, or even push the pace on. When you begin to sing the song, you mustn't lose this natural response to the poem.

As you speak the words, you will notice that the dynamic and dramatic range is quite small and controlled. Emphases are subtle, rather than strongly marked.

If you allow yourself to believe in the words and feel the sentiments as your own, contrasts **will** be created and your performance will be convincing.

Vocal exercises

Here are some vocal exercises to help you when you start to sing the song. They will 'warm up' your voice and, by using extracts from the song itself, will ease you into the technique required by your voice to produce the sound you would like to hear. Don't worry if you can't read the written music; the tape will play all the notes for you.

Check now that your posture is good (refer back to chapter 2). You should feel natural and relaxed, yet poised, with your torso well supported by firm stomach muscles and a comfortable, well-balanced stance. Feet a little apart, one slightly in front of the other. No tipping back from the waist, weight balanced evenly on the balls of the feet. Hands soft. Shoulders loose.

Concentrate first on producing a clear, round and focused tone. No wasted breath gushing out and no forced, anxious wobble. The tongue must be nimble, so that the sound continues like one bow stroke on a violin. Use a note that falls within the middle range of your voice. As with all of the exercises, try varying the pitch, always keeping within a comfortable range.

EXERCISE 1.1

'Le...le...la...'

Le... Le... La....

Switch on the tape now and first listen to the exercise before you practise it yourself.

Songs are usually sung in musical phrases, as speech is spoken in sentences. You must always sing through to the end of a musical phrase, rather than allow it to collapse, or die away. A musical phrase is like an arc of sound. You may want to snatch a silent breath during a long phrase and that's fine, but keep the musical sense of the phrase intact. The song will sound disjointed if you interrupt the flow of music every time you take a breath.

If you listen to the beginning of 'Morning has Broken' on the tape you will hear that there is a lot of vocal movement in the opening phrase. You do not want to have two voices; a strong and a meaty low voice and a thin, reedy high voice, so the next exercise helps you to balance the tone between the highest and lowest notes. Keep the low notes of the exercise clear and bright, so that they match up to the higher notes. Don't force the sound or it will become wild and wobbly. If you are really on the ball, using your breath efficiently and supporting the voice properly, you will make a full, bright sound. Say the words first, as if you were acting in a play, then sing them with the same realism. There is one note for each syllable to help you make a clean pitch change on each word.

Exercise 1.2

'Here she comes now, here she comes again'

Here she comes now here she comes a - gain

 Exercise 1.3

La———————————————————
Li———————————————————
etc.

When you feel confident that you are articulating the change of pitch cleanly, sing the same exercise without words, but using different vowel sounds each time.

There are several long notes in the song 'Morning has Broken' and it is important that you are able to sing them effortlessly, without the slightest hint of a wobble in your voice. Here is an exercise that will allow you to experience, then remember, the physical sensation created by a steady hum. As you open your mouth to vocalise fully, you should be able to sustain the same degree of control.

 Exercise 1.4

'Mmmmm...oh, mmmm...bro..., mmmm...broken'

mmm . . . . oh . . . . mmm . . . . bro . . . .

mmm . . . . bro . . . . ken

The word 'broken' takes you to the highest point, vocally speaking, of the song. Don't force the last syllable 'ken' because it is not the most important syllable of the word. Sing it gently and with an 'ah' mouth shape.

Now listen carefully to the tune you will sing on the tape. Play it through a couple of times before you begin to sing. Sing softly to start with, breathing in the proper places, so that you don't split a word or interrupt the natural flow of the music. When you feel confident, sing out, but don't expect to achieve a polished performance immediately. Find your way first and once you feel confident with the mechanics of the song, try again, this time imagining an audience seated at the other end of the room

Move the tape forward now to the piano accompaniment following on from the playing of the vocal line. Be in the mood; alert, gentle and charming, from the first note of the piece. Wait for the introduction. Don't draw in a long, planned breath. Breathe easily, spontaneously, just before you sing, exactly as if you were about to read a poem. Now communicate your song to your audience and charm them.

Spend at least one week using the vocal exercises in this chapter and considering the various aspects of singing generally, and this song in particular, before you take stock of your progress.

Even at this early stage, it will be enormously helpful if you can make a recording of your singing. Don't be too judgmental, or be tempted to abandon the recording altogether because you are frustrated or disappointed with the result. Date and keep the first recording, because you will feel an even greater sense of achievement at the end of the course if you hold some factual evidence of your improvement.

Morning Has Broken

Words by Eleanor Farjeon. Music by Cat Stevens

morn - - ing, praise for them spring - -
gar - - - den, sprung in com - plete - -

- ing fresh from the world.
- ness where His feet pass.

1. 2. 3.

4.

2. Sweet the rain's

7

LESSON PLAN 2
'The Sound of Music'

OBJECTIVES

More effective use of words.

Silently read through the words. Places to breathe are marked with a tick ✓.

Marks indicating optional breaths appear in brackets (✓).

My day in the hills ✓ has come to an end, (✓) I know.
A star has come out ✓ to tell me it's time to go. ✓
But deep in the dark green shadows ✓ are voices that urge me to stay. ✓
So I pause and I wait and I listen ✓ for one more sound, ✓
For one more lovely thing (✓) that the hills might say. ✓

The hills are alive ✓ with the sound of music, ✓
With songs they have sung ✓ for a thousand years. ✓
The hills fills my heart ✓ with the sound of music ✓
My heart wants to sing every song (✓) it hears. ✓
My heart wants to beat like the wings of the birds that rise(✓) from the lake to the trees. ✓
My heart want to sigh like a chime that flies ✓ from a church on a breeze. ✓
To laugh like a brook (✓) when it trips and falls (✓) over stones on its way, ✓
To sing through the night ✓ like a lark that is learning to pray.

> I go to the hills ✓ when my heart is lonely. ✓
> I known I will hear ✓ what I've heard before. ✓
> My heart will be blessed ✓ with the sound of music ✓
> And I'll sing once more.

—— **More effective use of words** ——

The main objective of this lesson is to make the most of the sung word. If there is variety in your singing, the listener will be kept interested and entertained. Variety can be introduced through dynamic contrasts, tempo changes, pauses or silence and by your treatment of the sung word. Once you have achieved control of your voice and can maintain an even balance of tone throughout the registers, the time has come to use your acting skills to enhance your presentation.

Read through the words of this song and you will realise why 'The Sound of Music' became one of the great success stories of the twentieth century.

Read through the words again and this time make a mental note of those you would like to enhance. When you begin to sing the song, you may feel that you would only like to give special treatment to one or two. That's fine. Your presentation of the song **should** be unique and has to feel right for you.

Your approach to this technique should be **subtle** rather than obvious.

Here are some suggestions for words you might like to enhance either with body language or with tone:

1 Don't stand staring up at the ceiling, because that would be crass, but a moment's glance into the middle distance would suffice for 'A star has come out to tell me it's time to go'.
2 The words 'deep, dark, shadows' would benefit from a suggestion of dark tone in the voice. Linger for the briefest moment over the 'sh' of 'shadows'.
3 When you sing 'I pause and I wait and I listen –' have a stillness about you that suggests you are doing just that.
4 Soften emotionally and physically as you sing 'one more lovely things that the hills might say'.

5   The direction on the printed copy – with warm expression – covers the opening section of the refrain. Feel even a little more 'up-beat' as you sing 'my heart want to sing every song it hears'.

6   So far your voice has sung largely in beautiful, smooth phrases. Now when you reach 'My heart wants to beat like the wings of the birds –', sing 'My heart wants to –' in this smooth, legato style, then break the vocal line as you sing 'beat/ like/ the' and emphasise the 'b' of 'beat'. Smooth again for 'wings of the birds'.

7   As you sing the word 'rise' imagine the birds soaring into the air and the tone colour will be right.

8   'My heart wants to sing –'. Emphasise the 's' of 'sigh' and use a little extra air as you sing the note.

9   You could extend the musical time given to the word 'flies' or alternatively give a little extra emphasis to the consonants 'fl-'.

10 Have a laugh in your voice as you sing the word 'laugh'.

11 As you sing 'falls' let your vocal pitch 'sigh' down **delicately** but make sure you sing the note perfectly in tune to start with, or it will sound terrible.

12 The penultimate emotion of the song is exhultation, but as it draws to a close, it pulls back from the emotional high and becomes contemplative. There is no big finish. The song occurs at the beginning of the show, setting the scene and the mood. Because it remains one of the main musical themes, as well as one of the best loved tunes, the implied promise contained in the final phrase 'And I'll sing once more' is enough in itself. Sing this final phrase clearly and fondly, with a slight crescendo on the final note.

These techniques can be adapted to suit any of your songs and once you become more adventurous with your interpretation you will be able to think of many more. **Never** overdo it and remember that once you repeat an effect, it ceases to be an effect and becomes the norm.

There is a lot to think about in this chapter. Once you have tried singing in line with the suggestions, you may feel that your own imagination has been stimulated to the point where you can toss aside most of the ideas, retain one or two, or mould them to fit better with your own understanding of the piece.

Go ahead, don't be frightened to experiment, it is natural to want to make every song 'your own'. You may really appreciate having the ideas in lesson plan two, because there are so many other things to think about, such as vocal quality and vocal control. **Lean on the suggestions for as long as you feel the need**. You are still at a very early stage in the course and until you feel confident that your voice is going to produce the sound you want to hear, anything that makes singing easier and more enjoyable for you is a valuable tool. The suggestions show you just how much can be done with a simple piece using breath, tone quality and body language.

Carry on using the vocal exercises in lesson plan one, as they are all concerned with helping you to produce the best sound possible. Add the vocal exercises from this chapter, listening carefully to every sound you make. Are you making the sound you expect to hear or must you try again, perhaps several times, before you are successful? Maybe a minor adjustment to your breath flow or mouth shape is all that is needed. Control won't come instantly, but it will improve if you keep trying.

——— Vocal exercises ———

Exercise 2.1

'Le, la, le, la'

Le.. La.. Le.. La.. Le.. La.. Le.. La.. Le..............

Make the 'l' sound with just the tip of your tongue. Flick it briskly while you send the voice forward in an unbroken stream of sound. Use the 'l' as a springboard onto the vowel sound. Be careful when you voice the 'l' that it is at the same pitch exactly as the vowel sound.

Exercise 2.2

'Ah, eh, oh, ee'

Ah.......eh....... oh....... ee....... ah

Don't 'dig into' the lower notes of each pair. The tone should be even and buoyant.

Exercise 2.3

'Ah, eh, oh, ee'

Don't overfill your lungs with air. Poise, mental energy and good support are vital to maintaining an even tone throughout this exercise. Remember to charm, or it may sound wooden.

Exercise 2.4

'Ah...ti, ti, ah...ti'

Make space for the 'i' vowel sound. Keep it round, rather than thin and tight. Make sure that the second time you sing 'ti', it is perfectly in tune.

Exercise 2.5

'Ah...ti, ti, ah...ti'

The tongue must be especially nimble. Imagine the vowel sound 'i' of the four 'ti's is one sound.

Always bear in mind other factors that can affect the quality of the sound you make, so don't become unreasonably impatient with yourself. Also, don't keep plugging away at the same point if things aren't going well for you. Return to an exercise or part of the song that you have enjoyed and feel confident about and sing it through. You can return refreshed to the problem at the beginning of another session, when you have had time to consider why it hasn't gone so well.

Each time you sing, try to end on a happy and confident note, so that you can look forward with pleasure to the next practice.

The Sound Of Music

Words by Oscar Hammerstein II. Music by Richard Rodgers

My day in the hills has come to an end, I

know. A star has come out to tell me it's time to

go. But deep in the dark green shad-ows are

hears._____ My heart wants to beat like the wings of the birds that rise from the lake to the trees. My heart wants to sigh like a chime that flies from a church on a

go to the hills when my heart is lone - ly.____

____ I know I will hear what I've heard be -

- fore.____ My heart will be blessed

mf più espressivo

8
LESSON PLAN 3
'If I Loved You'

OBJECTIVES

Pacing of the drama and dynamics of a piece.
To sing softly with clarity and carrying power.
To increase volume without forcing.

Read through the words silently first and then out loud as if rehearsing a part in a play. Places to breathe are marked with a tick ✓.

Marks indicating optional breaths appear in brackets (✓).

If I Loved you, ✓ time and again I would try to say ✓
All I'd want you to know. ✓
If I Loved you, ✓ words wouldn't come in an easy way, ✓
'Round in circles I'd go. ✓
Longin' to tell you, ✓ but afraid and shy, ✓
I'd let my golden chances ✓ pass me by! ✓
Soon you'd leave me, ✓ off you would go in the mist of day, ✓
Never, ✓ never to know ✓
How I loved you, ✓ if I loved you. ✓

Here is a character who is afraid to admit he or she is falling in love, so although your feelings may be deep and passionate, you can't be too aggressively assured in the way you sing the song. The melody is strong and persuasive from the very first note, but to maximise the effect of the song, allow all your passionate thoughts and responses to ebb and flow, just as they would in real life. If you don't have this contrast in your singing, your audience will become numb and unresponsive.

'If I loved you' offers an opportunity to demonstrate several facets of good singing technique. These, together with your emotional response to the music, will add a real showstopper to your repertoire.

Pacing of the drama and dynamics of a piece

One play through this tune is enough to show you that having built the drama in one section you must pull it back otherwise you will have nowhere to go, dramatically, or dynamically, by the end of the first page!

Rather than use volume alone to convey passion, consider intensity, emphatic consonants, word-painting, even introspection. With this last suggestion the whole song could be considered to be 'thinking aloud' with the audience allowed to intrude, but you will be 'singing out' to the audience for most of the time. If you at some point pull away your eyeline and, with the **smallest**, **most subtle** movements, draw in your body, temporarily losing the expansive, wide-shouldered feeling, you close yourself off, dramatically speaking, from the audience, even though still directing your voice out to them. In this way you can create a dramatic emphasis of the most potent yet subtle kind.

Feel the uncertainly, the vulnerability, the fear of rejection beneath the passional declarations of the singer.

Here is just one suggestion for a dramatic strategy. Using all the skills you have built up, you will be able to vary these suggestions and add more of your own.

1   Take the first section, 'If I loved you, time and again I would try to say all I'd want you to know'. Everybody knows and loves this tune, so state it, and the sentiments which you have made your own, clearly and warmly.

2   Show your vulnerability in the second section, by singing a little softer but with intensity, 'If I loved you, words wouldn't come in an easy way'. Slow down a fraction as you admit, 'words wouldn't come in an easy way'. Back to speed as you declare 'Round in circles I'd go'. Build the passion you feel and allow the volume to build too, as you sing the word 'go'. Feel that the music is pushing on to the next word 'longin' so that the word 'go' almost joins onto 'longin'.

3   'Longin' to tell you but afraid and shy'. 'Longin' is the high point, both dramatically and dynamically. Bring both these back, with some **subtle** shift of body language for 'afraid and shy'.

4   'I'd let my golden chances pass me by.' Build the volume, but keep it controlled. Emphasise the 'g' of 'golden' and the 'ch' of 'chances'.

5   Right back dramatically and dynamically for, 'Soon you'd leave me, off you would go in the mist of day'. Don't forget to appreciate lovely phrases such as 'mist of day'.

6   'Never, never to know'. Build, but don't belt. Emphasise the 'n' of the second 'never', rather than build volume from the first, otherwise you will be locked in a huge crescendo that can only end in an ugly sonic boom.

7   'How I loved you.' Intensely, with slight emphasis on the 'h' of 'how'. Float the 'oo' of 'you'. Linger on the word 'you' as you would linger on thoughts of the beloved.

8   'If I loved you.' Simply, with great warmth and sincerity.

To sing softly with clarity and carrying power

You may find several points in this song, as well as many others, where this is a necessary skill.

If you think about the use of soft speech and the difference between clarity and mumbling, you have already established a useful criteria for effective soft singing.

The tone must be as focused as ever. No excess breath or loss of energy. The effort required to sing softly and effectively leans towards using more energy rather than less.

The voice begins in the mind, so if you think 'here comes a soft passage, I'll back off and murmur', the only one to receive the song's message will be you.

Think instead about attracting someone's attention without disturbing others. Marshall all of your forces and focus them into one intense beam of sound, which you then deliver with concentrated energy.

Make it a custom to sing your exercises at a moderate volume and then as softly as you can. Don't swallow the sound, make it beautiful and tender and send it forward, like a beam of light, to reach the furthest seat in the gallery of the theatre in your mind.

– To increase volume without forcing –

Very occasionally, it is necessary to make a sound so loud that your whole body is consumed with effort. If you must do this for the sake of the drama, make sure that you release the tension immediately after your note and do not anticipate the tension in any way. Generally, overloud singing is ugly. Many people have loud voices, but the secret of success lies in harnessing that power and using it as just one of many attractive features of your voice.

Increasing volume begins in the mind, in exactly the same way as soft singing. Imagine a clear, penetrating sound; it may be warm, angry, passionate. You will colour the note with your innermost feelings. The voice is launched forward on a great burst of energy, never forced. As soon as you feel any discomfort in your throat, you are forcing the sound beyond your natural capabilities.

If you have a big voice and sing loud all the time, the audience cannot be expected to guess that you have any real artistic ability. If, on the other hand, you sing with subtlety and variety and can introduce volume with good taste at appropriate points in your performance, the audience will be entranced by your many-faceted talent.

Don't just 'turn up' the volume, always allow the real passion and intensity of a moment, controlled by your discriminating ear, to direct the volume of your voice.

Vocal exercises

 Exercise 3.1

'Ma, me, mi, mo, mu'

ma.. me.. mi.. mo.. mu..

Using the pure Italian vowel sounds, as described on page 19 in the Pronunciation chapter, make one strand of sound, like a bow stroke on a violin. Keep the volume moderate and the tone steady.

 Exercise 3.2

'Ma, me, mi, mo, mu'

ma.. me.. mi.. mo.. mu.........................

Use the 'm' to bring the sound forward. Get quickly onto the vowel sound and, while making a seamless sound, make each note distinct one from the other.

Take special care with your accuracy in the descending part of the exercise.

Feel your diaphragm working as you hold on to the last note, keeping your tone even and steady.

Exercise 3.3

'Ma, me, mi, mo, mu; ma, me, mi, mo, mu'

ma.. me.. mi.. mo.. mu.................
ma.. me.. mi.. mo.. mu.................
1) *mf*   2) ⟨ ⟩   3) **pp**

The exercise repeats, tempting you to breathe. Don't. Feel your diaphragm working, but do not allow yourself to tense. Learn to ignore any discomfort and concentrate on maintaining a good, steady tone.

Use the exercise at a moderate volume; at a soft, but distinct volume and lastly, allow the sound to swell and subside as you sing.

 Exercise 3.4

'La... pa, pa, pa'

As well as making a clear distinction between notes of different pitch and between your loud and soft singing, this exercise allows you to develop the techniques of both smooth, *legato* singing and *staccato*, short and detached singing. If you need to, take a breath before the staccato passage.

Use the same dynamic variations suggested in the previous exercise.

The musical phrases in this song are long and you must plan your breathing carefully, if the sincerity of the words is not going to be marred by your running out of breath.

Be sure that you are neither over-singing, nor over-breathing. Really believe in the sentiments of the song and be prepared to make substantial, if invisible, physical efforts to sustain the vocal line.

If necessary, go back to the chapter on breathing and remind yourself just how energetic an activity singing is. Are you really making enough effort?

You can appear variously bemused, hopeful, poised, eager, strong, or whatever the song requires, while concealing the fact that you are breathing with all the efficiency and energy of a long distance runner.

If you throw yourself in a controlled but wholehearted way into the very physical act of singing, you will be rewarded with success and the same buzz you would get from any other really demanding activity.

If I Loved You

Lyrics by Oscar Hammerstein II. Music by Richard Rodgers.

9
LESSON PLAN 4
'Somewhere'

OBJECTIVES

To achieve distinct, unobtrusive pronunciation.
To breathe effectively.
To sing high notes with confidence.

Silently read through the words. Places to breathe are marked with a tick ✓.

Marks indicating optional breaths appear in brackets (✓).

There's a place for us, ✓
Somewhere a place for us. ✓
Peace and quiet and open air wait for us somewhere. ✓

There's a time for us. ✓
Someday a time for us. ✓
Time together with time to spare, ✓
Time to earn, ✓ time to care. ✓
Someday, (✓) somewhere ✓
We'll find a new way of living, ✓
We'll find a way of forgiving, ✓ somewhere. ✓

There's a place for us, ✓
A time and a place for us. ✓
Hold my hand and we're halfway there. ✓
Hold my hand and I'll take you there, ✓
somehow, (✓) someday, ✓ somewhere.

To achieve distinct, unobtrusive pronunciation

This tender song is a good model to measure the clarity of your pronunciation. You can't over-articulate; it would sound ridiculous. You can't mumble either, because lovers want to hear what each other has to say.

There **are** potential pitfalls within the text and you will find plenty of similar examples in your other songs.

Watch out for:

'There zah place foruz';
'Peace and quie tan dopen nair';
'We'll finda new wa- yof living'.

Good pronunciation is a subtle skill and should be so unobtrusive that it doesn't affect the musical line, or the sense of the words.

Read the words to yourself. Say them out loud. Finally, sing the song 'under your breath', listening intently to make sure that your sung words have not become mangled and comical, instead of intense and moving as they should be.

The secret is not to allow your consonants to bleed onto words where they don't belong. Some blending is possible, even desirable, where a gentle, crooning affect is required, but if you apply that technique carelessly you will lose the thrust of the prose and a beautiful song will become ugly.

To breathe effectively

'Somewhere' is like a piece of dramatic prose. It isn't just a pretty tune inserted to decorate the drama, but an integral part of the plot of the musical 'West Side Story'.

Learn the words as you would a part in a play. Say them out loud expressively, adding a word or two if it feels more natural to you. When you feel confident with your spoken performance, repeat it, this time listening to your breathing. Do you snatch a breath at one point? Do you take a breath like a sigh? Do you breathe silently and spontaneously in response to one section? Is there a point where you draw a sharp, voiced breath? How about transferring your breath plan for the spoken words to the song. Does it work, or will you have to adapt it in some way?

You may feel snatched breaths are appropriate in the middle section beginning, 'Time together...' where the music builds and the excitement grows. Then breaths more like sighs as the music and drama subsides again. With practice, you will find a method that suits your style and pace of singing.

Singers learn to breathe silently by not tensing the throat muscles, which brings the vocal chords together causing the breath to be voiced. Generally, silent breathing is what is required, but now that you are working on a dramatic song, rather than a singing or breathing exercise, don't be afraid to use the sound of different types of breathing to add to the drama.

– To sing high notes with confidence –

Go over to the mirror reading to sing a note that you consider high.

Stop... Just before you make a sound, what do you see? Anything in your face that isn't alert and happy is wrong. Madly quirked eyebrows, furrowed brows, muscles standing out on your neck, screwed up eyes, tense jaw, bared teeth, etc. etc. etc.? All **wrong**.

Muscular effort is required to sing and more effort is required to sing some notes than others, but the tensing of muscles occurs an instant before the note is produced and relaxes when the sound ends.

To colour your high notes with passion or to make a rock sound, or to shout takes a lot of effort, but be sure you're not over-working your throat; engage the whole body, just as you would if you were going to yell.

Good, clear high notes can be produced using far less effort than you might imagine. When you really go for an unusually big sound, as mentioned above, several things happen automatically. To produce a better quality, smaller sound in the high register, think of some of the things that happen when you go for the biggest noise possible:

- it takes a lot of effort from the whole body, not simply one area;
- you feel a rush of energy;
- the buttocks tense;
- you open your mouth;
- the soft palate is arched;
- the sound is catapulted from your mid section, not the throat;
- the throat opens to allow the sound to be launched forward on a burst of energy;
- you feel a real buzz on your cheekbones and eyes.

Making good quality sounds isn't so different. In fact, although you might want to look more poised, you would use all of the same physical and mental efforts. Of course you would monitor the quality of the sound more closely, using your listening skills to produce the best sound possible at the level of volume you want to hear.

If things still aren't going well, ask yourself if it's simply your **attitude** to high notes which is causing tension and blocking them. High notes and low notes do need more attention because they are notes you don't use very often, but that doesn't mean that you can't sing them, only that you must allow yourself time to become accustomed to the new physical sensations and be patient as you slowly develop your ability to sing throughout a wider range with confidence.

- Use the exercises to help you to develop the muscles you will need to support the sound.
- Be patient, it may take months, rather than minutes, but if your energies are engaged correctly, you should find that your progress is far more exciting than you dared to expect.

Vocal exercises

 Exercise 4.1

'Ma, me, mi, mo, mu'

ma.. me.. mi.. mo.. mu............

Using the pure Italian vowel sounds discussed in the chapter on pronunciation, let the sound be an uninterrupted stream, the lips moving briskly together and apart to form the 'm'.

Don't swoop' from one note to the next. They are joined, yet pure and distinct from each other.

All the vowel sounds should balance, so that one does not stand out from the others. For example, a thin or harsh 'i' sound would leap out from the rest.

Exercise 4.2

'Mu, ma, me, mi, mo, mu'

mu. . . . . . . ma.. me.. mi.. mo.. mu

Reverse the sounds. Again watch for smooth yet distinct transition between each note, with an even tone quality throughout the exercise.

Exercise 4.3

'Now sing for joy'

now sing for jo - - - - - y

An 'open-shouldered' feel to this exuberant exercise. Aim for an even and clear tone quality from top to bottom of the range. Take care that the top note does not become wild. Pitch it carefully, so that the descending scale can be absolutely in tune.

Work to attain the same degree of accuracy you would expect from any other instrument.

 Exercise 4.4

'Joy'

Use this exercise to develop your accuracy further.

Use the 'j' of 'joy' as a springboard onto the vowel sound, but don't allow the 'j' to be too aggressive.

Keep the vowel sound pure right to the end of the exercise and then finish with a neat 'y' rather than an ugly 'yuh' sound.

It will help you to gain confidence in producing free and full sounding high notes if you begin some exercises at the top rather than always working up from the bottom of your range.

 Exercise 4.5

'a, e, i, o, u'

This exercise will increase your confidence for producing and sustaining high notes.

Begin at a pitch where you feel you can create a good tone and where you can sing easily.

As you move the exercise to a higher pitch, make sure that you don't introduce tension, because this prevents the production of good top notes.

If you don't **believe** that you **can** sing high notes, you will tense up every time and prove yourself right!

Energy, not tension, and lots of self-belief, will give your voice the best chance to show what it can do.

The highest point of the song 'Somewhere', 'We'll find a new way', is made more awkward by the 'ee' vowel sound which occurs on the highest note. If you say the word 'we'll' you will notice that you hardly need to open your mouth at all, but when you sing, you **must** open your mouth. Don't tighten the mouth and pull it to either side. Instead, drop the jaw open gently, making a fuller 'ee' sound. Be snappy with the 'w', arriving quickly onto the vowel sound. Open your mouth into an 'ah' shape as you sing 'ee':

'Think 'ah', sing 'ee'.'

 Exercise 4.6

'We'll... We'll find a...'

The same technique applies to the 'i' vowel in the word 'living' and again in the word 'forgiving'. Don't make the sound too thin and reedy. Allow the jaw to drop gently so that there is some space in the mouth for the note to resonate. Once again, the consonants should be brisk.

 Exericse 4.7

'i...i...living'

Sing the song through and experience the drama. Feel the music and project it out, so that you could draw an audience into the plot.

'Somewhere' requires lots of the invisible energy so often mentioned in this book. Many of the phrases begin quite softly, but the pick up of each phrase must be firm, even if the volume is very low indeed. In just the same way that you sing through to the **end** of a phrase of music, the **start** of each phrase must be sure.

You will be singing long phrases, so aim to maintain a good balance of tone colour throughout the vocal range and pace the drama carefully.

If you sing too slowly, you will lose the innocence of the song and the sentiments will become heavy and studied.

If you sing too fast, you will make your emotion seem superficial and the poignancy will be lost. Pace rather than speed keeps the appeal in the song urgent, without foreshortening the wonderful suspended phrases.

Make sure that you are familiar with the section on high notes so that you don't squeeze, tighten or force them.

A gentler, focused sound can be *more* penetrating, and *more* affecting than any careless blast of sound.

'Somewhere' reveals the character's vulnerability in a desperate situation. There is no aggression and your choice of tone quality should reflect these sentiments.

Don't worry if you have to experiment with note production until you are satisfied with the sound you are making. You have the exercises to help you and you can spend all the time you need. Remember that tone quality depends on how you feel and how you transmit those feelings. Believe in the words and let the music bring out your acting skills.

Somewhere

from *West Side Story*

Lyrics by Stephen Sondheim. Music by Leonard Bernstein

There's a place for us, Some - where a

place for us. Peace and quiet and

op - en air wait for us some - where. —

There's a time for us, Some - day a

time for us. Time to - geth - er with

liv - ing,_____ We'll find a way of for - giv - ing,_____ some - where._____

There's a place for us,

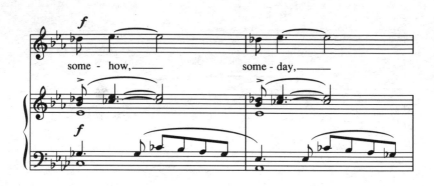

some - how,_____ some - day,_____

1.

rall.

some - where._____

2.

some - where._____

10

LESSON PLAN 5

'Take me to your heart again' ('La Vie en Rose')

OBJECTIVES

To produce good low notes.
To balance the sound between higher and lower registers.
To sustain an even and unforced tone throughout a line of repeated notes.
To be able to benefit from the relaxation of vocal muscles.
To convey the intensity of the song without either vocal or dramatic forcing.

Silently read through the words. Places to breathe are marked with a tick ✓.

Marks indicating optional breaths appear in brackets (✓).

Take me to your heart again, ✓
Let's make a start again, ✓
Forgiving and forgetting; ✓

Take me to your heart again, ✓
And leave behind from then, ✓
A life of lone regretting. ✓

Dearest, let's turn back the years, ✓
Let smiles come after tears ✓
Like sunshine after rain. ✓

I'm yearning for you (✓) by night and by day, ✓
Praying I'll soon hear you saying ✓ 'I love you', ✓
Then we'll never part again, ✓
If you will take me to your heart (✓) again. ✓

Anyone who heard Edith Piaf sing this song could not help but be affected by her huge personality and plangent voice; her passionate interpretation is unforgettable. Fortunately, most of us can only guess at the harsh experiences which could produce such intensity, so don't attempt to copy Piaf but make the song your own. It is passionate, but keep the emotion under control and at an appropriate level for you. The melody is beautifully lyrical and the sentiments of the song receive emphasis through the repeated notes in the last section.

The vocal line must not be allowed to sag at any point and the whole piece requires a great deal of energy and careful pacing of both drama and dynamics. Read through the words before you begin, this time out loud. It should be possible to say the words in almost the same time that you will sing them.

Good low notes

Have you ever thought about the pitch of your speaking voice? It is probably close to sung notes which you consider to be 'low'. In other words, you are using this register all the time, so don't be frightened of it.

Low sung notes must be kept clean, direct and as natural as speech:
- no excess breath
- no hooting
- lift and brighten the sound so that the notes have focus
- Don't make the sound too heavy or it will not blend with your higher register.

Vocal Exercises

 Exercise 5.1

'Grey skies'

Take a pause each time you sing the exercise or you will lose the spontaneity. Imagine yourself glancing out of a window and commenting to a friend in a matter of fact voice 'grey skies'.

 Exercise 5.2

'Grey skies'

Move the voice now. If you make the sound too heavy, your instrument will lose its flexibility. Don't have a solemn expression on your face, or the sound will be ponderous. With a pleasant, if rueful expression sing, 'grey skies'.

To balance the sound between higher and lower registers

The voice should be steady, clear and direct with no swooping between the two notes and a good balance of tone quality between the registers, i.e. not too heavy down below and not too weedy on top.

Here is an idea that will help you. Imagine you are standing in front of a class of naughty seven-year-olds. Clearly and authoritatively, but without shouting, you are going to say, 'late again!'. Now sing the same phrase with exactly the same mental picture in mind.

Vocal exercises

 Exercise 5.3

'Late again'

 Exercise 5.4

'Ah, no'

A gentler version of this exercise will lead you into the technique required to handle the leaps in the song. As you sing the phrase, colour the sound with a thought – sad, irritated, apologetic, for example.

'Ah, no; ah, no'

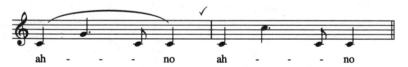

 Exercise 5.5

Phrase building: 'And for-'

Exercise 5.6

'For-get-ting'

for - get - ting   for - get - ting   for - get - ting

Exercise 5.7

'And for-get-ting'

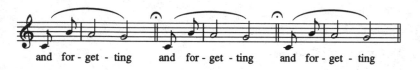

and for - get - ting   and for - get - ting   and for - get - ting

Exercise 5.8

'For-giv-ing'

for - giv - ing   for - giv - ing   for - giv - ing

Exercise 5.9

'For-giv-ing and'

for - giv - ing and   for - giv - ing and   for - giv - ing and

Exercise 5.10

'Forgiving and forgetting'

for - giv - ing and for - get - ting   for - giv - ing and for - get - ting

This technique can be used with tricky sections from any of your songs.

To sustain an even and unforced tone ‾throughout a line of repeated notes‾

Energy, energy, energy and no forcing, or the music you create will become ugly and, in time, your voice could be damaged. Feel the emotion deep inside yourself, but remember that as a performer you must remain in control at all times

Exercise 5.11

'I'm yearning for you'

I'm yearn - ing for you   I'm yearn - ing for you

Exercise 5.12

'By night and by day'

by night and by day   by night and by day

Exercise 5.13

I'm yearn - ing for you   by night and by day

'I'm yearning for you by night and by day'

Pace the line carefully. Say the words, so that you feel the natural emphases. When you sing the line, don't forget you can use consonants for emphasis as well as volume. Break the phrase into two parts to start with.

To be able to benefit from the ___ relaxation of vocal muscles

There is a split second when you have sung the word 'day' in exercise 5.7 where you can allow your vocal muscles to relax. If you adopt this technique, your voice will reap great benefits.

Much vocal strain is caused not simply by over-singing, but because the vocal muscles are kept in a state of tension throughout a performance.

If you consciously review what is happening when you sing a high note, you will find that there is some necessary tension. Problems occur when you anticipate the tension, setting it up too soon, or when you fail to relax the muscles when a suitable opportunity occurs. It is easier to spot general physical tension, yet overlook the problem where it affects the singer most – in the throat.

Exercise 5.14

'By night and by day. Praying I'll soon...'

by night and   by day   pray - ing   I'll   soon.

* Shorten 'day' slightly; relax tension; breathe; continue.

Join the whole phrase together as you complete the phrase; sustain the mental poise and remember the physical sensations required to keep the vocal line, as you allow your muscles to relax for an instant, then breathe, set up the correct physical state and move on to the next phrase, 'Praying I'll soon hear you saying 'I love you'.

To convey the intensity of the song, ——— without either vocal ——— or dramatic forcing

This is far more more complex song, both emotionally and vocally, than, say, 'Morning has Broken', and it will help you to have a plan in mind before you begin to sing.

Keep your physical poise and vocal buoyancy all the way through the song. Use the singing exercises to 'warm up' your voice and to deal with specific areas in the song, then listen to the tune on the tape several times while you consider the following points:

1 Use the 't' of the opening word 'Take' to launch cleanly onto the vowel sound. Have the note in your mind as you make the 't' a little more explosive than usual.
2 The second time you sing, 'Take me to your heart again', try plaintive rather than forceful.
3 Caress with your voice the word 'Dearest'.
4 Encourage the imaginary recipient of your song with the phrase 'Let smiles come after tears'.
5 A little push on to persuade further with the phrase 'Like sunshine after rain'.
6 Not too loud with 'I'm yearning for you'. Emphasise the 'y' of yearning instead.
7 Soften emotionally and dynamically to sing the word 'Praying'.
8 Break before 'I love you'.
9 Emphasise the word 'love'.
10 Float the 'oo' of 'you'.
11 Emphasise 'n' of 'never'.
12 Sing the final phrase in one breath as far as 'If you will take me to your heart'.
13 Linger over 'again'.
14 Keep poise up to and beyond the final note. This is a dramatic song and you can suspend the drama for a moment or two beyond the last note.

Up to now, the lessons have largely been concerned with developing your listening skills, your technique and your interpretation. Just to check that all that concentration and intensity of purpose isn't swamping your natural urge to get up and sing, it is time to bring back the mirror.

- Make sure you don't overact, or pull funny faces.
- Tell your story convincingly
- Watch out for physical quirks.
- Enjoy yourself!

Try to use a mirror for some, if not all, your practice sessions. You can be both performer and audience, with the mirror taking the part of a really helpful teacher.

Take Me To Your Heart Again

(La Vie en Rose)

E. Piaf / Louiguy

CHORUS

Take me to your heart a-gain, Let's make a start a-gain, For-giv-ing and for-get - - ting;

Quand il me prend dans ses bras, Il me par-le tout bas, Je vois la vie en ro - - se,

Take me to your heart a - gain,
And leave be - hind, from
Il me dit des mots d'am - our
Des mots de tous les

then, A life of lone re - gret - ting.
jours, Et ça m'fait quel - que cho - se,

poco rit.

a tempo

Dear - est, let's turn back the years,
Let smiles come af - ter
Il est en - tré dans mon coeur,
Un - e part de bon -

tears   Like   sun - shine   af - ter   rain.
- heur,   *Dont*   *je*   *con - nais*   *la*   *cause,*

poco più mosso

I'm yearn - ing   for you   by night and   by day,
C'est   *lui*   *par*   *moi, Moi*   *par*   *lui, dans*   *la*   *vie*

mf

Pray - ing   I'll   soon hear   you   say –ing   'I love   you,'
Il   *me*   *l'a*   *dit, l'a*   *ju - ré pour*   *la*   *vi - e.*

11

LESSON PLAN 6

—— 'Day Trip to Bangor' ——
('Didn't we have a lovely time')

OBJECTIVES

To sing fast with accuracy.
To leap easily from one register to another.

Read through the words several times; there are a lot of them! Then, read the words out loud and in rhythm. Snatch a breath where you can, always keeping the rhythm strong, as well as keeping the sense of the words.

Didn't we have a lovely time the day we went to Bangor,
A beautiful day, we had lunch on the way and all for under a pound.
You know that on the way back I cuddled with Jack and we opened
    a bottle of cider,
Singing a few of our favourite songs as the wheels went round.

Do you recall the thrill of it all as we walked along the sea-front?
Then on the sand we heard a brass band that played the Tiddley-
    pom-te-ra-ra.
Elsie and me had one cuppa tea then we took a pedalo boat out.
Splashing away as we sailed round the bay as the wheels went
    round.

Wasn't it nice eating chocolate ice as we strolled around the fun-
fair?
Then we ate eels on the Big Ferris Wheel, we sailed above the
ground,
But then we 'ad to be quick 'cos Elsie felt sick and we 'ad to find
somewhere to take her.
I said to the lad, what made her feel bad, was the wheel going
round.

Elsie and me, we finished our tea and said goodbye to the seaside.
Climbed on the bus, Flo' said to us, 'Oh isn't it a shame to go?
Wouldn't it be grand to 'ave cash on demand and to live like this
for always?
It makes me feel ill when I think on the mill and the wheels go
round.'
Ya da da deedle da da da da deedle da da da da.

From the sublime to the cor blimey! And why not? Although I think a
Northern accent would be better, if you can do one. This is an excellent example of a contemporary folk song, marked with great humour,
good spirits and strong rhythm. Get the words in; all of them tell the
tale clearly and with a swing.

—— To sing fast with accuracy ——

The fact that there is usually one word or syllable per note in this
song will help you to sing fast. You can use the consonants to bounce
the rhythm along.

But before you put the words and music together, sing along to one
sound 'pa'. This will help with your musical accuracy before you combine the dozens of words with rapid scales and equally rapid leaps.

This technique will help you with any fast vocal passages. The 'p' consonant reminds you to 'bring the sound forward' and ensures that you
articulate every single note clearly instead of unwittingly swooping
between one or two, as you might if you used a vowel sound alone.

Practice plan for singing rapid passages

1 Sing fast passages at a slower tempo using 'pa'.
2 Bring up to speed using 'pa'.
3 Sing the proper words or vowel sounds of your song slowly.
4 Bring the proper words or vowel sounds of your song up to speed.

 Exercise 6.1

'Pa pa pa pa'

Enjoy the clarity this simple device provides. Each note is produced accurately and the slight emphasis on each beat of the bar helps to bounce you along. Eventually you will feel confident enough to do without the emphasis on each beat and will be able to sing smoothly and accurately without the 'p' to help you.

To leap easily from one register __ to another

 Exericse 6.2

(Couplets) 'Pa, pa, pa'

Slight emphasise on the first note of each couplet. Clarity on the second, higher note. This exercise is buoyant and flowing.

Exercise 6.3

(Triplets) 'Pa, pa, pa'

pa pa pa *etc.*

As with the previous exercise, to begin with use a slightly emphasis on the first note of each triplet to help you pitch correctly. Eventually you can lose this emphasis and the consonant 'p'. When you reach this stage, experiment with different vowel sounds.

Exercise 6.4

'Day we... day we..., went to... went to..., day we went to..., day we went to...'

Day   we   Day   we   Day   we

Exercise 6.5

'Went to'

Went   to   Went   to   Went   to

Exercise 6.6

'Day we went to'

Day   we   went   to   Day   we   went   to

Listen to the phrase, 'Day we went to Bangor...'. The words you would emphasise in speech are, 'day... went... Bangor' and so they remain when you sing.

Sing the lower notes without any pressure and at a level that will balance with the higher notes. The high sung words, 'we, and, to,' are not stressed and should 'ping' like bells. Be buoyant and energetic in your mind and body, and the springboard will be in place for your vocal leaps.

Take the song verse by verse to start with. Keep your energy levels high; this is always important when you sing and even more so when you have such a busy piece to put across. Make each entry firm and bounce the words along. Let yourself rip with this song. You have worked hard and deserve some fun!

You may not always find this the easiest song to sing. Your energy levels **do** have to be high to sustain a good singing tone throughout the piece and you may not always feel in the mood, either vocally or in a more general sense. That doesn't mean you can't sing anything.

In the same way that you would **listen** to different music according to the time of day, occasion or how you happen to be feeling, so it is with your choice of song. You are free to choose. Unless you have a sore throat, pick another song. You have covered quite a variety of styles and speeds of singing now and should be able to find the right piece of music to suit your mood.

Do come back to the song when you are feeling refreshed. It is sheer entertainment and fast moving; something new to add to your growing catalogue of skills.

Day Trip To Bangor

(Didn't We Have A Lovely Time)

Words and music by Debbie Cook

all for un - der a pound. You know that on the way back I

cud - dled with Jack and we o - pened a bot - tle of ci - der,—

Sing - ing a few of our fa - vour - ite songs as the wheels went

round.

Do you re-call the thrill of it all as we walked a-long the
Was-n't it nice eat-ing cho-co-late ice as we strolled a-round the

sea-front? Then on the sand we heard a brass band that
fun-fair? Then we ate eels on the Big Fer-ris Wheel, we

played the Tidd - ley - pom - te - ra —ra. El - sie and me had
sailed a - bove the ground but then we had to be quick 'cos

one cup - pa tea then we took a ped - a - lo boat out.
El - sie felt sick and we 'ad to find some- where to take her.— I

Splash - ing a - way as we sailed round the bay as the
said to her lad what made her feel bad was the

wheels went round. Did - n't we have a
wheel go - ing round.

lov - e - ly time the day we went to Ban - gor,— a

beau - ti - ful day we had lunch on the way and all for un - der a

pound. You know that on the way back I cud - dled with Jack and we

o - pened a bot - tle of ci - der,_ Sing - ing a few of our

To ✛ Coda

fa - vour - ite songs as the wheels went round.

El - sie and me, we fin - ished our tea and said good - bye to the

sea - side.— Climbed on the bus—— Flo said to us, 'Oh,

is - n't it a shame to go.' — Would - n't it be grand to 'ave

cash on de - mand and to live like this for al - ways? It

makes me feel ill, when I think on the mill and the

wheels go round. Ya da da dee - dle da

da da da dee - dle da da da da.

12
LESSON PLAN 7
'Amazing Grace'

OBJECTIVES

Unaccompanied singing.
Accurate singing.
Breaking the silence.
Rhythm.
Interpretation.

Silently read through the words, then read them out loud.

Places to breathe are marked with a tick ✓. Marks indicating optional breath appear in brackets (✓).

Amazing grace, how sweet the sound ✓ that saved a wretch like me. ✓
I once was lost, ✓ but now am found; ✓
Was blind, ✓ but now I see. ✓

'Twas grace that taught my heart to fear ✓
And grace my fears relieved. ✓
How precious did that grace appear, ✓
The hour I first believed! ✓

Through many dangers, toils and snares ✓ I have already come. ✓
'Tis grace hath brought me safe thus far ✓
And grace will lead me home. ✓

When we've been there ten thousand times, ✓
Bright shining as the sun; ✓
We've no less days (✓) to sing God's praise ✓
Than when we first begun. ✓

—— Unaccompanied singing ——

Don't panic at the thought of singing unaccompanied. You have probably done far more already of this type of singing than you imagine
and there are ways for you to tighten up your skills, ensuring that
your listeners hear what you want them to hear.

Accurate singing

Accurate singing is a must. You want to be sure that your audience is
hearing what you think and hope they are hearing.

1 Learn the song thoroughly before you sing without accompaniment by listening to the tape that accompanies this course.
2 Think the song through in silence, to make sure that you really
 are familiar with every part.
3 Sing the song through partly accompanied, partly unaccompanied.
 Use the second version of your tune on the tape. It will be played
 in strict time, with some parts missing. If you keep on singing
 through the silences, you will be able to tell how accurate you are
 when the music restarts. Don't worry if you don't sing the whole
 song correctly right away; you can always go back to the complete
 tune on the tape and practise any parts you find tricky.
4 To reinforce the technique used in point 3, play the second version
 of the tune through again. This time, don't sing during the
 silences, but continue the song in your head. When the recording
 starts again, you begin to sing too. You will find out how accurate
 you are pitch-wise and rhythmically, but remember that this is an
 exercise and allow yourself a little leeway as far as the rhythmical

interpretation goes. You should be absolutely accurate when it comes to hitting the right note, of course!

If you were learning lines for a play, you might expect to make one or two slips to start with and these last two exercises are no different. The more you use your musical memory, the more reliable it will become.

Breaking the silence

Breaking the silence takes courage. When is the right moment? Don't rush. If you are in front of an audience, wait for them to settle, so that you have their attention. Look happy and confident, feel poised and calm. Run through the opening phrase silently in your head, to establish a speed, then count yourself in, again in your head.

Rhythm

Rhythm is an element that may be overlooked in unaccompanied singing because, in the same way as with the pitch of the song, there is nothing to keep you in line. You must feel the rhythmical pulse of the piece and communicate that assurance to the listener. Don't cut notes short unnecessarily, or ignore any rests and pauses that you might expect to observe if you were singing with an accompaniment. There is a natural break at the end of each verse. Don't rush on through it, but observe it so that you keep the rhythmic content and balance of the whole piece intact. This is not to say that you can't highlight a word by drawing out its timespan, or that the whole song should be sung in relentlessly strict time. Some degree of personal interpretation is both welcome and necessary. As in accompanied singing where, strictly speaking, the accompanist follows the singer, use the given notes and rhythm of your song as a skeleton that you flesh out with your own informed and unique approach.

Interpretation

Interpretation in unaccompanied singing has to take into account the fact that there are no distractions whatsoever. Just pure, undiluted you, so keep your voice and your thoughts focused and disciplined. It is more important than ever that you do not lose concentration for even a moment.

The real benefits of being a singer come into their own with unaccompanied singing. Unlike some other musicians, you have always got your instrument handy and can enjoy making music free of charge, any time you want to!

Vocal Exercises

By this stage you will want to develop your vocal range and stamina. Don't breathe in the middle of the next two exercises, or you will inhibit their flow. You are listening for an easy and even tone. The notes are close together and though you want them to flow smoothly, each is accurate and does not 'bleed' into the next sound. You should hear an evenness of quality in your voice now from top to bottom of the range.

 Exericse 7.1

'Ma, me, mi, mo, mu...'

 Exercise 7.2

'Ma, me, mi, mo, mu'

Exercise 7.3

'Mu, mo, ma, mi'

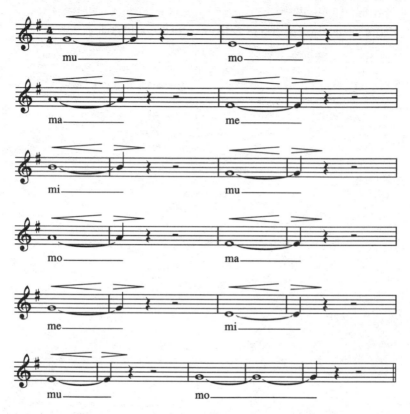

mu——

mo——

ma——

me——

mi——

mu——

mo——

ma——

me——

mi——

mu——

mo——

Clarity and control are needed to begin a note softly, swell and then subside again without losing a good and even tone. The secret of unaccompanied singing is starting off at approximately the right pitch. If you know the song well, as you must, you will know whether the first few notes are the highest you are going to have to sing, or whether the high notes come later in the piece. This knowledge decides your choice of opening note. There is nothing more horrendous than beginning well, only to find that the end of a song has soared out of reach!

- Err on the side of caution; you can always take up the ending for an impressive finale.
- If something feels easy and comfortable to you, it probably sounds good to your audience.

Make your aim to charm rather than to impress

If you find you have any remaining problems with your singing, there should be a section in the book that can help you. Choose exercises from any of the lesson plans that you think can best help. Don't be afraid to compose some of your own exericses, or take sections from the songs and use them to continue building up your technique.

Amazing Grace

TRADITIONAL

once was lost but now am found; Was-
grace hath brought (✓) me safe thus far And

blind, but now I see. 'Twas-
grace will lead me home. When-

grace that taught my heart to fear And-
we've been there (✓) ten thou - sand years, Bright-

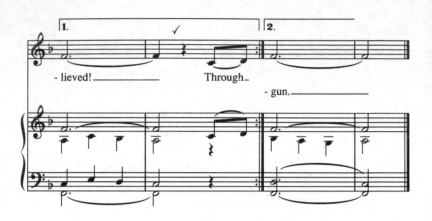

- lieved!_____   Through_

- gun._____

Part Three

DEVELOPING YOUR SKILLS

13
— FINDING A TEACHER —

If you are keen to develop your interest in singing further, the time may have come to find a teacher. An objective appraisal of your potential should be helpful and most music colleges offer consultation lessons, as do many singing teachers.

Don't commit yourself hastily to a teacher, because an approach that suits many others may not suit you. Sometimes it is necessary to try several different teachers before you find one with whom, instinctively, you feel you can develop a rapport. You are entitled to expect the teacher of your choice to provide inspiration, encouragement and expert guidance to direct you along a path which will best foster your development. You should be prepared to accept constructive criticism and be aware of the fact that creative impetus cannot be one-sided. You must respond in equal part to the energy the teacher devotes to you.

A teacher should be flexible. Teaching is about communicating, and a blanket method cannot suit everyone. Any music lesson, by its very nature, must always contain some element of spontaneity, but a lesson which drifts on without structure or purpose is no use to you.

Having found your ideal teacher, don't expect instant results. Tape your first lessons and then make another recording about six months later. By this time some improvement should be noticeable.

Find a reputable teacher through your local music shop, college or reference department of your local library, where various groups, such as ISM (Incorporated Society of Musicians), will have listings of teachers in your area.

When you find a teacher, it is up to him or her to set an appropriate pace for learning, and to make sure that every lesson is a mutually enjoyable experience. A teacher who points out your weaknesses at every opportunity will chip away at your confidence.

You want a teacher who can build on your strenths, and find ways to tackle problems without destroying your self-belief and confidence.

14
OLDER AND YOUNGER VOICES

———————— **The older voice** ————————

It is never too late to sing but, like a rusty door hinge, an older voice that hasn't sung for many years will need some attention before it is ready to work again. Don't rush into technically demanding songs, or try to impress with what might be, even though long neglected, a big sound. The road back to vocal fitness should be travelled steadily and with patience.

If you live alone and don't use your voice as often as you would like, you may have lost, even in your speaking voice, many of the variations of pitch, tone colour and emotional response which used to be present. All the more reason to take up singing. Buy some music you really enjoy listening to and sing along. Ask yourself what it is that you find particularly appealing about the voice of the singer you have chosen. It is unlikely to be the sheer power of the voice. Apart from being attracted to a particular style of music, you will probably identify a special quality, the individual charm of the singer. Everyone possesses an unique vocal quality which reflects their innermost being in sound. The singer works towards making that sound as appealing as possible. If you rely on power alone, the listener will quickly become numb and unreceptive. If, at the other extreme, you feel that you have lost the power of your voice, or it trembles uncontrollably, gain control again through speech. Speak aloud the words of your song.

Become used to hearing yourself speaking clearly, charmingly and at a volume above the level of polite conversation.

Sustain words where the rhythm of the song demands. Feel your diaphragm working. Singing is an energetic activity and you will need to put in a lot of effort. Once you become used to the physical sensations, you will be able to forget them and get on with the business of making music.

Like a young voice, the older voice must train sensibly, at a steady pace. The tone colour and range may have changed over the years, but look on that as an opportunity rather than as a handicap. Experience will lend a quality of authority to your interpretation and you may be able to explore some entirely new repertoire. You may find that different parts of your voice require working on now, so be prepared to create an entirely new routine for yourself, rather than falling back on an old method. Choose a simple song to start with, one that is well within your capabilities and one with which you can identify. Think about the words. Say them out loud, Break the song into phrases and satisfy yourself that you can sing each phrase convincingly before you attempt to put the song together. Make your presentation, if only for your own benefit, as natural and as charming as possible. Stand well, relax and aim to be a convincing story-teller. Don't oversing, or overdramatise. A simple, honest presentation is always the best. The song should have a dynamic and a dramatic framework which you never abuse. A sudden loud note, or an isolated and overly dramatic gesture, would abuse this framework and spoil the effect of the whole piece.

Is the tone good throughout, or have you sacrificed good tone for the sake of a loud passage? Never sacrifice good tone for anything other than comedy, or some other special dramatic effect. Emphases that are far kinder to the listener can be achieved in better ways. A sharp intake of breath, an explosive consonant, any of these is preferable to a sudden, unbalanced trumpeting.

Use controlled breathing to keep the voice steady. Build up the technique gradually, using the exercises in the relevant section of this book. Wobbles can be controlled and, in time, eliminated, if you use the smooth, legato vocal exercises regularly. Listen carefully while you practise to make sure that the voice really is steady and keep your air flow at a constant rate as you sing each note. The big vibrato which used to be the signature sound of many singers is not longer admired. Vibrato is a useful device to add warmth and effect, rather as a string player might, but a constant gurgle only irritates or even amuses the listener. Your singing should appear to be as natural an activity as speaking. Enjoy what you sing and the audience will enjoy it with you. Give the best of yourself and they will love you for it.

——————— The younger voice ———————

Joining a choir is one of the very best ways to introduce a child to singing and a good director of music knows how to select music that is not going to strain tender young voices. The most successful type of training scheme usually includes vocal exercises, together with a broad education in musicality and technique.

Choral singing demands team work and discipline, but the rewards are great. Even the most timid child will get a chance to express emotions freely, meet new friends and perform in front of an audience.

Good singing requires energy and enthusiasm, qualities that children possess in abundance. There are no restrictions, special requirements or financial demands, such as the purchase of an instrument, so everyone can have the chance to make music.

Teachers vary in their opinion regarding whether or not children should be taught to sing. Of course children should be taught to sing; whether they should have their voices 'trained' depends upon what is implied by the word, trained.

However exceptional a young voice might seem, the temptation to force or push should be avoided at all costs.

The range of a child's voice increases gradually; its tone colour mellows and matures as the child grows older. These qualities should be allowed to develop naturally, without pressure from ambitious individuals.

A good teacher can assess a child's voice and will respect the limitations. At the same time he or she will remain alert to the child's development and will be able to respond accordingly.

Childhood presents a valuable opportunity for the singing teacher, an opportunity diminished by the inhibition that maturity brings. If children are allowed to experience a wide variety of style, drama, texture and dynamics, they are more likely to carry through to adulthood an adventurous approach to music making.

Although children may appear to have great extremes of pitch range, if you consider a sulky mutter in the lower register, or an angry screech at the top end of the range, neither of these extremes is normally sustained for long and they should not be exploited in singing.

As a general rule, it is better to choose songs that fall within a range of little more than one octave, at least to begin with. Even within that apparently small range, fun pieces are plentiful.

Don't be over-cautious with the choice of song. Children enjoy and rise to the stimulus of a challenge and quickly become bored, if they think that they are being seriously underestimated. If their skills and imagination are never tested, they will never know what they can achieve.

Training a voice, which involves regular and progressive exercise, should not be started until the young voice has settled, and this applies to girls as much as to boys. Around the age of sixteen or seventeen, this type of training may become appropriate, although each individual must be assessed carefully by an experienced teacher.

Some voices do not mature, or settle, until the singer is well into his or her twenties, but at each state of development there will be songs that are appropriate.

Even children as young as eight or nine can be taught the principles of good singing. This should involve lots of fun, basic musicianship, learning to sing accurately and in tune, sight-singing, learning to breathe properly, appreciation of words and poetry, clear diction, clean vowel sounds, understanding, singing to the end of phrases, presentation skills, thoughtful interpretation, careful listening...

None of these will damage a young voice, but can only be to a pupil's advantage, whether or not they decide to continue singing when they are older.

There is always a danger that a talented youngster might be swept up by a professional or amateur group, where their voice is exploited and over-used, with no regard for their long-term prospects. Don't allow your child to become 'cannon fodder'.

The quality of a damaged voice may be lost for good, or it could become so unbalanced that the top end of the range is weakened and useless, in comparison to the few over-used low notes in the speech/shout range. The consequence of this type of misuse will mean that the child finds it impossible to make the transition from cute 'belter', with a few note range, to mature, lyrical singer, with a wide-ranged and well-balanced voice.

Of course, children can sing in shows both successfully and safely, but they must build up their vocal stamina carefully over a period of time and learn to conserve their voices whenever possible, for instance miming in rehearsals, when their part is covered by others, and only turning up the volume for the minimum time required. If they are only using part of their vocal range in the show, their daily exercises should concentrate on that part of the voice which is not being used, finishing each session with an exercise that uses the whole range, just to make sure that a good balance is being maintained throughout the voice.

15
– PERFORMANCE SKILLS –

For many people, this book will lead towards a very tangible goal: a public performance. That performance might be a full-blown public appearance, or it might form a crucial performance element in a music examination.

Whether amateur or professional, there is only one way to approach such an event with confidence and that is to be well prepared both musically and organisationally. Always remember:

- You want to be a success.
- You want to enjoy the experience.
- You want to learn from the experience.
- You want to be asked to sing again.

Know your audience

The best way to achieve success is to know what your audience wants and then to give them something more. That audience might be one adjudicator at a festival or examination centre, your friends at a social gathering, chums down the pub at a Karaoke evening, or the spectators at a public performance. If you want to feel confident and relaxed, your approach should be the same for each. You will always feel a *frisson* of anticipation if you care enough about your singing, but if you are well prepared you will be able to tolerate the pre-performance butterflies, freeing the artistic side of you to enhance your performance.

Audience mix

As with any other group of people, the mix of personalities making up an audience remains broadly similar. Of course they are on your side, or they wouldn't be there, but on every occasion expect to find:

- the carping critic
- the ignorant sleeper
- the gentle listener

Of course you hope for a majority in the last category, but the sooner you accept the presence of the other two, the easier it will be for you to accept the pressure of performance.

This is not a new concept, but one that was familiar to performers as far back as Renaissance times. Performance then was viewed as a multi-level pyramid. Each layer of that pyramid represented a specific

Performance Pyramid

Figure 10 Elements present at every performance

participant, or group of participants, at their rightful level in the art of performance. Putting things in perspective like this will help you to rationalise many of the fears and concerns regarding performance that can be built up for no good reason.

————— Your programme —————

Try to achieve a good balance to your programme. Sometimes it helps to work to a theme which will help to focus your thoughts and make the choice of music easier. The occasion itself might suggest a theme which would have relevance and appeal to your audience. Of course you should 'play to your audience', but you should also please yourself. Enthusiasm is infectious and an audience is more likely to respond positively if you are enjoying the performance.

If you want to incorporate a deep and meaningful or unusually popular song in your programme lead your audience towards it, don't drop them in it right away. You must create a mood in order to achieve the maximum impact and you can help this along with your choice of material leading up to the pivotal song.

Once you have evoked a certain emotion, don't jerk the audience out of the mood you have worked so hard to create. Work back gently onto a lighter plane.

By taking care over the planning in this way you will allow yourself, as well as the audience, time to prepare for the change of mood.

Singing to pre-selected music

If the music you are to sing has been selected for you, study it carefully using the guidelines discussed throughout this book. If possible, listen to recordings of singers whom you admire, singing the same or a similar style of song. If you can listen to several different recordings, so much the better. This is not so you can copy any particular version, but it does allow you to hear subtle and sometimes not so subtle variations between one recording and another. Listening to several performance possibilities may inspire you to try something new.

The Venue

If you can, visit the place where you are to perform and have a good look round. Your walk on-stage from the dressing room, from your seat in the audience (in the case of a festival, for instance), or down the side of the stage, will be much easier and hopefully hazard-free if you have scouted the area properly in advance.

What are the acoustics like? It would be ideal if you could have a rehearsal, but this is not always possible.

Check for blind spots and locate the best position to stand for your performance. Form a partnership with your accompanist, so that he or she can hear you, and vice versa. Don't stand centre stage if the piano, for instance, is situated to one side. On the other hand, don't restrict yourself unnecessarily by standing pressed up against the piano, because your performance space is all around you, as far as you can reach up, down and around.

Music Festivals

Your audience will almost certainly have paid for their seats, so you will need to observe all the etiquette of performance: dress smartly, take care with your general grooming, *perform* to your audience, and remember to acknowledge their applause with a simple bow once your song is over.

When your number or name is called, leave your seat and walk up to the front. It is not always wise to take up your performance position immediately. The adjudicator may still have comments to write concerning the previous competitor. Keep your eye on the adjudicator and be ready to take up your position as soon as he or she has finished writing. In the meantime, you could go through the music silently with your accompanist. If you are to sing unaccompanied, stand to one side, or do not mount the stage until you can see (or have been told) that the adjudicator is ready for you.

If the title of your song is not shown in the programme, announce the name of your piece, and its composer, before you begin to sing.

When your class has been judged, be gracious both in victory and defeat. You are entitled to be thrilled if you win, but don't gloat. If you don't do as well as you expected, or hope to, bear in mind that the judgement is one person's opinion, but one to which he or she is entitled. Read the adjudicator's comments carefully; you may find the observations invaluable. Most adjudicators are trying to be supportive and to give you good advice which will help you to improve your technique and the general level of your performance skills.

Don't discuss your fellow competitors in an unkind way; you might be sitting next to a relative! Learn from the experience and, without bitterness or regret, look forward to your next music-making opportunity.

Auditions

Be realistic about auditions. Use them for experience by all means, but remember that the people auditioning you may have a very clear idea of the sort of person they are looking for. If you are not successful, it may be that you do not fit into that particular pigeon-hole, vacancy or even costume.

You may feel apprehensive, but the auditioning panel will understand. They will be looking to see how you cope with the pressure of an audition, as this will give some indication of how you will respond to the pressures of performance. A ready smile helps to put **them** at ease.

Your audition piece should have relevance to the part you hope to play or cover, and it is always wise to learn more of the part, just in case you are asked any related questions.

Know your music so well that if the pianist accompanying you stumbles, you can carry straight on without the slightest hesitation. If you are not allowed to bring your own accompanist, make sure that your music is in a good state of repair and clearly marked up where you intend to repeat or cut a section, or where you feel that the printed directions do not fully express your musical intentions. If you have the opportunity to do so, speak to the accompanist and make those intentions doubly clear before you begin. Once the music has started you cannot stop to ask for the tempo to be made slower or faster.

If you think one might be required, prepare a neat one-page cv on good quality paper and take along a head and shoulders photograph. Above all, be professional in the way you prepare yourself for an audition and in the way you conduct yourself throughout.

Examination

You may be entered for an examination by a friend, a relative or even by yourself, but it would be wiser to seek the advice of an experienced and well-qualified teacher before you do so. Song preparation must be scrupulous and there may be other elements that count towards the final mark, such as aural tests, or sight-singing.

You may have to perform your examination pieces in a small room, in front of one person; this can be a little off-putting. Imagine that beyond the examiner is your audience. You glance would not remain static and staring, but would 'work the audience'. You should include the examiner in this glance from time to time, but no more than you would include any other member of your 'audience'. Send your voice forward easily, out to that 'audience' beyond the walls of the small room. Make your contrasts clear and unaffected and don't rush between songs, or between any of the various elements of the examination.

———————— Dress code ————————

Appearance is a critical element of your performance, since judgements based on visual evidence are already being formed before you utter a sound.

Check the appropriate dress code for every performance and also enquire about use of colour, as your best pink dress might not look so good against bright orange curtains, for instance. A blunder such as this can be extremely distracting for an audience.

Make sure that you have no restricting items around your throat, for instance, a tight collar, tie, necklace or scarf.

Some actors like to build a character 'from the feet up'. Whatever your choice of footwear, make sure it is not only suitable for the occasion but comfortable and, most important of all, doesn't clatter as you walk across the stage.

— Singing in a professional capacity —

If the choice of music is left up to you make sure you know your audience. In a concert setting, it will not be possible to 'read a room' as a band-leader might. In this situation, you will need to know in advance the likely make-up of your audience.

You must contact the organisers of the event and ask them some questions:

- Length of programme required.
- Number, age and type of audience.
- Size of venue.
- Type of accompaniment to be provided/or not.
- Will you need band or orchestral parts, or will they be provided for you? Make sure, if you are using your own copy, that you are using the same edition of the music as everyone else. A piece of music can vary quite considerably between one edition and another.
- Dress code.
- What facilities will or will not be provided for you backstage. If you are singing with a backing tape, make sure that the accompaniment is going to follow the same order of verse, chorus, etc, that you are expecting to hear.
- Don't be afraid to ask the organisers for suggestions: you are not obliged to follow their ideas rigidly.

Organising Yourself

As soon as you receive a reply to your questions, open a file in which you can keep correspondence, contact names, addresses, telephone numbers, music and any other paperwork that is relevant. Label the file showing the date, place and time of the event and keep it somewhere safe.

——————— Interpretation ———————

Convincing interpretation requires attention to detail, imagination and acting skills. Rather than imitate another singer's work, communicate the sentiments of each new piece as your own either remembered or imagined experience.

To stand alone and sing takes courage and the ability to sustain a mood without costume, scenery or the interplay between two or more characters. Emotions are shown in facial expression, body language and vocal colour. If your face is expressionless, you are not believing the words you sing. Facial expression relies on genuine emotion and inner conviction. Be natural, rather than exaggerated.

Theatrical gestures are out of place anywhere but the theatre.

A song's mood is set before the first note of the introduction and the song does not end until the final silence after the last note. You are 'in character' for every moment of that time. Rests and pauses are all part of the music and you must not lose concentration during them.

What do you know about a song? What do you hope to communicate? When you know what it is, convey your message with authority. When you walk on-stage, your mind should be full of the mood of your first song; you are already creating an appropriate atmosphere. If you are singing several songs of different character, give yourself time to experience the new mind-set each time you sing.

A happy and charming expression colours the voice beautifully. Melancholy and drama also have their place, but, however briefly, let light shine into the darkest mood. Monotony can set in if one emotion is sustained throughout a piece. Contrast, however subtle, is an essential element in retaining the interest of the audience. Great extremes of emotion can easily miss their mark and amuse the audience, when you intended them to be touching. When you have learned a piece, plan a dramatic strategy in your mind and ensure that all your emotional responses fall within an appropriate scale. Your reactions to a piece should appear totally spontaneous, although you may have them worked out broadly in advance.

Talent and inspired intuition is not enough. Hard work is needed to 'flesh out' the character you will become when you sing.

—————— **Microphone technique** ——————

When you transfer your performance from the rehearsal studio to the stage, get to know the workings of all the items you will encounter during your performance.

If you find that a microphone stand has been placed incorrectly, or has been adjusted too high or too low for you, you will need to be able to make any necessary adjustments swiftly and apparently effortlessly, so that you don't distract your audience. If you want to lift the microphone from the stand at some point, make sure that you clear the stand right away from your performance area. You don't want to be dodging around it during your song.

If you have some very loud passages to sing, or alternatively will be singing for any great length of time, remember the microphone is there to catch your sound as you project the voice, therefore you should not be singing 'to the microphone' unless to create some intimate moment or special effect. By projecting the voice beyond the microphone and not forcing the sound *at* it, you will be less likely to tire or strain your voice.

Don't point your microphone directly at a speaker or you will cause howling 'feedback'. Always have a sound check before a performance and ask someone who can make constructive comments to listen to you. Even using a monitor, you can gain a false impression of the sound the audience will hear.

All the rules concerning extended vowel sounds and compacted consonants become irrelevant, because you can alter or enhance your sound simply by adjusting a setting. As long as your speakers are powerful enough and well placed, your audience will be able to hear perfectly.

─────── After the performance ───────

Control your natural euphoria and don't do or say anything that you might have cause to regret later.

Accept and learn from criticism, though evaluate it in the context of the person who makes it. Ask yourself whether they are speaking from a position of knowledge combined with a desire to help and inform, or for some other, less worthy motive.

Accept praise with a simple 'Thank you'. No lengthy expositions or, 'Didn't you hear my cracked note in bar 70?' And no darting eyes, seeking out a more interesting flatterer.

On a practical note, keep a record of what you have sung, where, and what you wore. Any peculiarities or problems that cropped up that you might forget in time, or confuse with another time and place, can also be noted.

What did you like about your performance and where did you feel there was room for improvement? Make every performance a learning experience.

Finally remember that a performance is only one day in your life; you can neither live on it, nor fail by it.

The 'Spontaneous' Song

Now you are a singer, people may ask you to sing for them at the most unexpected moments. The best piece of advice to ensure you are never caught out is **rehearse your spontaneous song in advance!**

16
OVERCOMING STAGE FRIGHT

A degree of apprehension is acceptable for both the professional and the novice and is, to some degree, the consequence of possessing a sensitive and artistic temperament. You care about your work; you are anxious to do your best. But don't allow your thoughts to roam unchecked. The possibility that you might forget your words, repeat the wrong bit of a chorus or dry up altogether will transform an acceptable level of keyed-up anticipation into emotional incontinence.

Control the situation; don't allow the situation to control you. Fear is not acceptable. Fear is a result of ignorance, lack of confidence and poor preparation. All of these have a solution that lies within your range of influence. There are simple precautions you can take to ensure that you are armed with confidence:

- Check through Chapter 15 on Performance Skills.
- Prepare all your work in a detailed and thorough manner.
- Double check that you are using the correct editions of each work to be performed.
- Be orderly in your business dealings.
- On the day of performance, don't allow yourself to be rushed or distracted.
- Practise relaxation skills before a performance.
- Put yourself in control of everything within your sphere of influence.

People in the theatre have always been famous for superstitions and pre-performance rituals. Laying out stage make-up, props and personal items in the dressing room in a particular order is a favourite. Integral to this seemingly quirky behaviour is a consistent pattern and with this pattern comes order: an ordering of thought and a calming certainty that you have everything under control. Many years ago, the Romans used this same order-inducing pattern principal in their speeches. The rules of rhetoric demanded that a speech be planned according to a specific format. Major sections of a speech were likened in the mind to stages in a journey.

If you apply this strategy to your performance, the imaginary journey could be tailored to fit the length and pattern of your programme. Each stopping-place would reveal a vista or an object chosen by you to represent a new song in your mind.

In the quiet time that you allow yourself before a performance, you can retrace the steps of your imaginary journey, soothing your mind, while, at the same time, using the deep-breathing exercises to calm your body.

If remembering parts of a song is your greatest worry, you will find that most songs contain a pattern. Identify and memorise that pattern. Your memory will develop with regular use in the same way as the voice.

Everyone suffers from 'nerves' to a greater or lesser degree. In at least one of the major British conservatoires a sick bucket is placed at the side of stage for use by Diploma candidates, so you are certainly not alone in feeling this way, but do be sure that your 'nerves' are not an excuse for either an ill-prepared programme or a manifestation of pride, at the thought that you will never be able to demonstrate just how wonderful you really are.

Be warm and polite, rather than agitated and prickly; make friends generally with your surroundings, so that they feel familiar to you and you feel comfortable with everything and everybody; you don't want any little surprises to come along and disturb your focus.

Finally, offer yourself unreservedly as the medium through which the composer's intentions will pour. Be generous and eager to share your gift. Every time you make music it should be a celebration, not a trial.

17
— YOUR REPERTOIRE —

Familiarity and personal preference are likely to influence your selection of music in the early stages of your study, but don't be afraid to explore new material, or even take a fresh look at previously discarded songs.

Consider the character of a song as well as its technical demands, remembering that your facility for role playing will develop as you become more experienced.

Make a note of each new song in a repertoire book. This will make it easier for you to put a programme together at a later date. You could adopt a number of strategies for keeping a record of the songs you know. To begin with, a simple list will do, but once that list begins to grow, some page headings could make your records more accessible. The headings might read, Musicals, Pop, Dance, Country and Western, Folk, Humorous, for example. Alternatively, you could make listings under the names of specific composers. Your repertoire book is also the place where eventually you might keep a record of where you have sung, what you sang, what you wore, and any other notes pertaining to the performance.

If you are aiming to create a cabaret act, you should be thinking in terms of building 'sets'. These are groups of pieces that last for approximately twenty minutes and can stand either as individual programmes or be linked together to form a longer presentation. Singers working regularly in clubs and hotels must be prepared to provide music for dancing, which again should be grouped by type. This might include rock 'n' roll, country and western or pop, for instance. Be prepared to perform your songs in strict time for sequence and ballroom dancing.

You will be able to sift through a wide selection of popular music and songs from shows at your local music shop.

Further ideas for your repertoire can be obtained by reading the syllabus of one of the several music examination boards. Here you will find a sound selection of music for all levels of student singer. You can obtain these lists free of charge in all sheet music shops. Song selections are shown in voice type and are graded by degree of difficulty.

If you were put off singing as a child, don't spurn the songs of childhood now. Some of them have stood the test of time because they are tuneful and fun to sing. If you learn to sing them accurately and with pleasure, you will be reinstating the confidence of which you were robbed. A collection called 'Sing Together!' contains a good selection of this type of song.

'Twenty Four Italian Songs and Arias', a collection of Arie Antiche, is used by most of the leading conservatoires as a foundation repertoire for its student singers. Many of these early Italian songs have great appeal and put to use the vocal techniques being developed by the singer.

To give you an idea of what is available, the following pages outline some different musical styles.

——— Styles and applications ———

Barbershop

Barbershop, a close harmony style developed in the United States, combines the best of vocal technique and discipline with sheer entertainment.

In the sixteenth century British barbers amused themselves between customers by playing instruments or singing. This spontaneous music-making had almost disappeared by the early part of the eighteenth century, because more profit could be made from wig-making, but the association between music-making and barbers' shops travelled West. Before hot and cold running water became the norm in every house, men gathered daily for a shave at the barber's shop, as well as for the occasional hair trim. Whether customers burst into song with sheer delight at the sight of their clean-shaven faces, or whether quartet singers were employed to entertain, is not known for certain. What we can be sure about is that this highly developed style of American folk art continues to grow in popularity. The four vocal parts are still known by their traditional names – tenor, lead, baritone, bass – and a distinctive feature of the style is that the 'tenor' sings a harmony line above the melody of the 'lead'.

This follows early American hymn singing tradition, where men sang the hymn tune, while the women sang a harmony line above. Barbershop singing is a cappella, that is to say, unaccompanied. If you enjoy the camaraderie of choral singing, are eager to develop your technique and enjoy the pizazz of show business, Barbershop might be just the style you have been looking for.

Choral singing

Numerous groups of singers who perform together exist nationwide. It is important for you to find a choir or chorus, where you feel comfortable with your fellow choristers, the personality of the musical director and his or her choice of music. The wonderful thing about choral singing is that the sum of the whole can far outstrip the abilities of the individual. A cautionary note that would also apply to singing in the chorus of any show or opera is to be careful not to oversing. Remember that your voice has been chosen to blend with a whole section, rather than outstrip the volume of the person standing next to you. If your section is directed to sing louder by the conductor, you should sing a little louder and not force your tone to match someone who may have a far more powerful voice.

Country and western

Originally known as Hill-Billy, this is one of four forms of music native to the United States, the other three being Barbershop, Dixieland jazz and the Spiritual. Born of the cowboy song and the folk music of rural southern United States, until the 1920s country music was largely performed at social gatherings. With the advent of the radio and gramophone the style developed, becoming more commercial and less regionally based. After the Second World War, Nashville, Tennessee was heralded as the capital of country music, which was now performed and enjoyed worldwide.

The style may have broadened, but the themes used in the songs remain a constant reminder of the raw emotions that touch everyday lives. The vocal treatment required for these songs reflects their gutsy and direct content.

Early music

Songs of this era are usually performed using a pure and largely vibrato free vocal line. A repeated chorus would require some ornamentation or addition to the written vocal line in keeping with the general musical style of the piece. The intelligent and sensitive delivery of the words is as crucial to the composition as good singing, since the marriage of poetry and music was thought in the Renaissance era to possess special powers which could move the soul of the listener. Frequent long musical phrases demand excellent breath control and the preferred voice type would be light, well-focused and flexible.

Folk singing

Folk singing comprises those songs which are part of a community's oral tradition. They are passed on, yet may be enhanced, embellished or exist in several variants. Individual interpretation of the given material is part of the tradition. The vocal delivery can be harsh and cutting or lyrical depending on the dramatic content of the piece. Folk singing is strong in rural communities with a tradition of cultivated music.

Gospel

Gospel is used to describe the style of American revivalist religious song which succeeded the spiritual song in the late nineteenth century. The music is characterised by lively rhythms and simple harmonies. The vocal style is robust and emotional, with the best singers possessing a well-developed technique, honed over many years of sincere and thoughtful performance. Together with individuals, church congregations and choirs the Salvation Army, founded by William Booth in 1878, has helped to popularise this style of music worldwide.

Hymns

Hymns, in a similar way to singing the national anthem, bring together like-minded people in a celebration of song. The unifying force of words, music and physical effort is uplifting and refreshing bringing focus and a sense of purpose and belonging. St Augustine, 354–430 AD, defined a hymn as requiring three elements. '– praise, praise of God, and these sung'.

Jazz

Jazz singing requires the ability to use the voice with exactly the same independence as any other instrument. Improvisation, a feel for 'swing', the ability to bend then return a note to pitch, experimenting around a given rhythm, are among the skills required.

Karaoke

Karaoke singing follows on from 'Music minus one' which was a series of recordings available for the classical musician. These recordings were complete in every detail of accompaniment, the only missing element being a soloist.

The pleasure of performing to a professional backing tape obviously had commercial possibilities. The Karaoke phenomenon has provided every age and style of singer with the opportunity to perform to tapes that closely cover the most popular recordings. Comparisons with the original artiste may be amusing or even impressive, making this style of singing enormously entertaining.

Lieder

The term *lieder* (songs) is usually used to describe those songs of the Romantic era of music, roughly between 1790 and 1910. The voice forms an equal partnership with the accompaniment, creating a union between music and poetry, together with dramatic characterisation and scene setting.

Musicals [Musical Comedy]

Plays set to music, often containing spoken dialogue, demand a natural and fluent delivery. The works of Gilbert and Sullivan, European operetta, British Burlesque and Music Hall all contributed to the heritage taken up by such American composers as Jerome Kern, George Gershwin, Cole Porter and Irving Berlin in the 1920s and 1930s. The name, musical comedy, suggests easy listening, dance and glamour and perhaps gave way to the more contemporary word, 'musical', with the opening of Leonard Bernstein's 'West Side Story'. This show has a sophisticated score and a dramatic plot, based on the tragic theme of Romeo and Juliet. Stephen Sondheim, who wrote the lyrics for 'West Side Story', and Andrew Lloyd Webber continue the tradition which has become one of the most popular art forms of the twentieth century. Although amplification is used generally in modern musicals, it would be unwise to imagine that an untrained voice could cope with either the customary heavy scheduling of both amateur and professional productions, or with the sometimes demanding vocal writing.

Music Therapy

Music sometimes possesses the power to communicate when other methods may have failed. The rhythms of music echo our body rhythms, making them familiar, yet at the same time intriguingly different. The world is full of sound which can be confusing to those who cannot easily sift and evaluate the many strands. Music brings order to that chaos of sound and with order comes reassurance. Once contact has been established, involvement can be encouraged and developed.

Among the many therapeutic applications of music therapy, people who have suffered strokes and now have speech difficulties can sometimes be helped by using song or intoning. This therapy is known as Melodic Intonation Therapy. The theory behind this type of treatment is that it seeks to make use of the unimpaired right hemisphere of the brain, which is though to be involved in 'automatic speech', music and singing. Chanting or singing short sentences in unison with a therapist or helper, progresses until the person can sing or chant unaccompanied. The Stroke Association has produced a Singalong tape and a songbook to complement this therapy.

The Guildhall School of Music and Drama, the Roehampton Institute and the Nordoff-Robbins Music Therapy Centre are among several academic institutions offering post-graduate training in this discipline.

Opera

To equip your voice with the stamina necessary to sing opera, you must exercise it regularly, preferably under the supervision of a qualified teacher.

Technique should be developed alongside stamina, so that the voice has flexibility and subtlety, as well as power. Interpretation skills must also be nurtured, so that the voice possesses the power to move, as well as the power and focus to reach the back row of the gallery without amplification.

Acting skills and familiarity with stage-craft are essential to an art form which is now less stylised and more realistic than ever before. Good health and fitness are also pre-requisites for opera, because of its physical demands. Opera styles vary enormously, so once again, it is important for you to find a group that sings the type of work with which you would like to become involved.

Pop; Cabaret/Crooning

With the advent of the microphone it became possible to sing as softly as a murmur, yet reach out effectively to an audience. Many different effects and vocal textures which are not usually at the disposal of the singer can be produced using artificial amplification.

Spiritual

A type of folk song tinged with melancholy, yet trusting in a joyful after-life; or a rhythmical work song, of which Black spirituals constitute the largest surviving body of material and are probably the best known. Early published works were entitled *Spiritual Songs* to distinguish them from the hymns found traditionally in church use. The Jubilee Singers of Fisk University, Nashville, Tennessee, first performed a programme of Black spirituals to a large audience in 1871, and from this time their popularity as a concert item grew apace.

As their general popularity grew, so the spirituals lost favour with church congregations and were supplemented by the Gospel style. The 'call and refrain', still used today, recognises its African origins. Spontaneous and improvised song results when a congregation takes up a line from the preacher and gives the sentiment further weight and consequence through song. The White spiritual is also closely associated with the eighteenth century Baptist movement and nineteenth century revivalism. With close ties to folk song, the White spiritual embraces religious ballads and folk hymns.

GLOSSARY

All words are Italian, unless otherwise marked: E – English; G – German; L – Latin; F – French.

TERM	TRANSLATION/EXPLANATION	ABBREVIATION
A	At, to, by, in	
A capella	(lit. In the church style.) Unaccompanied vocal music	
Accelerando	Gradually faster	Accel
Adagio	Slow	
Adagietto	A little faster than Adagio	
Adagissimo	Very slow	
Ad libitum (L)	With freedom	Ad. lib.
Affettuoso	With feeling; tenderly	
Affrettando	Pressing on	
Agitato	Agitated	
Al fine	To the end	
All 'ottavo	Play, or sing, an octave higher	8ve
Alla	In the style of	
Alle breve	Originally indicated four minims in a bar, now more usually indicates two minim beats in a bar	
Allargando	Broadening out	
Allegro	Bright and fast	
Allegretto	Fairly quick, but unhurried	
Amoroso	Lovingly	
Andante	At a moderate walking pace.	
Andantino	Either a little faster or a little slower than Andante	

TERM	TRANSLATION/EXPLANATION	ABBREVIATION
Anima	(lit. Soul.) *see* Con Anima	
Animato	Animated	
A piacere	At pleasure	
Appassionato	Passionately	
Aria	A vocal solo, either independent or part of a larger work such as an opera or oratorio	
Arietta	Short aria	
Arpeggio	The sounding of the notes of a chord one after the other, rather than together	
Assai	Very	
A tempo	Back to the original time	
Attacca	Attack	
Ballad	A song. Sometimes each verse is sung to the same tune	
Barcarolle	(lit. A boat song)	
Bel canto	(lit. Beautiful singing) The classical style of singing which originated in Italy in the 17th century. Characterised by effortless technique and beautiful tone	
Ben bene	Well	
Ben marcato	Well marked	
Berceuse (F)	Lullaby	
Bewegt (G)	With movement	
Bis (L)	Twice	
Bocca chiusa	(lit. Mouth closed, i.e. humming)	
Bravura	With spirit	
Breit (G)	Broad	
Brillante	Brilliant	
Brio	Vigour	
Cadenza	A florid and brilliant passage, usually for the solo performer and generally placed at the end of a piece. Used to show off technical skills. Some may be improvised by the individual, others are written out	
Calando	Dying away	
Calmato	Calm	

TERM	TRANSLATION/EXPLANATION	ABBREVIATION
Canon	A composition in two or more parts. The theme is introduced by one part, then taken up by subsequent parts	
Capo	(lit. Head.) The beginning. *see* Da capo	
Cantabile	In a singing style	
Cantata	A composition, sacred or secular, for voices and orchestra	
Canto Ferma	(lit. Fixed song.) For example, plain song or secular music with long note-values	
Canzona	Song	
Canzonet	A little song	
Cappriccio	Light-hearted composition	
Catch (E)	A round in which there is a play on words	
Cavatina	A short aria type composition	
Coda	(lit. Tail.) An added section, placed at the end of a composition, to make a good finish	
Colla Voce	(lit. With the voice.) A direction to the accompanist to follow the voice	
Come	As	
Come prima	As at first	
Come sopra	As above	
Comodo	At a convenient pace	
Con	With	
Con anima	Lively	
Con brio	With spirit	
Con espressione	With expression	
Con fuoco	With fire	
Con grazia	Gracefully	
Con moto	With movement	
Con spirito	Spirited	
Crescendo	Getting louder	Cresc.
Da.	From	
Da capo	From the beginning	D.C.
Dal segno	From the sign	D.S.
Deciso	Firmly, decisively	
Decrescendo	Gradually becoming softer	Decresc.
Delicato	Delicately	
Diminuendo	Gradually becoming softer	Dim.

TERM	TRANSLATION/EXPLANATION	ABBREVIATION
Di molto	Very much	
Dolce	Sweetly	
Dolente	Sadly	
Dolore	Grief	
Doppio	Double	
Doppio movimento	Twice as fast	
Duet	A composition for two voices	
Ein wenig (G)	A little	
En dehors (F)	Emphasised	
En pressant (F)	Pressing on	
En retenant (F)	Gradually getting slower	
Energico	With energy	
Espressivo	With expression	
Etwas (G)	Somewhat	
Facile	Easy	
Fermata	Pause	
Feurig (G)	Fiery	
Fine	The end	Fin.
Forte	Loud	
Fortissimo	Very loud	
Forzando	Forcing. A sudden acent	
Furioso	Furiously	
Giocoso	Happy	
Glee (E)	A simply harmonised, unaccompanied English song	
Glissando	A sliding effect, achieving a smooth rise or fall in pitch. *See* Portamento	
Grandioso	Grandly	
Grand Opera	A dramatic piece for vocal soloists, chorus and orchestra	
Grave	Very slow, solemn	
Grazia	Grace	
Grazioso	Gracefully	

In alt	Notes from ___ are said to be *in alt*	
In altissimo	Notes an octave higher than *in alt*	
Incalzando	Increasing speed	

TERM	TRANSLATION/EXPLANATION	ABBREVIATION
Lacrimoso	(lit. Tearfully.) Sadly	
Langsam (G)	Slow	
Largamente	Broadly	
Largo	Slow and stately	
Lebhaft (G)	Lively	
Legato	Smooth	
Leggiero	Lightly	
Leitmotiv (G)	A theme that represents a particular idea or character	
Lent (F)	Slow	
Lento	Slow	
Lied (G)	Song	
Light Opera	A dramatic piece for vocal soloists, chorus and orchestra, containing a certain amount of spoken dialogue	
L'istesso tempo	The same speed	
Lontano	As from a distance	
Lunga pausa	A long pause	
Lusingando	Coaxingly	
Ma	But	
Ma non troppo	But not too much	
Madrigal (E)	A contrapuntal composition for unaccompanied voices	
Maestoso	Majestic	
Mancando	Dying away	
Maggiore	Major	
Marcato	Accented	
Martellato	Fiercely accented	
Marziale	Martial	
Massig (G)	Moderate	
Masque	An early dramatic production combining poetry, music and dancing	
Meno	Less	
Meno mosso	Less movement	
Messa di voce	Expressive use of crescendo, then diminuendo, on a long note	
Mezzo-forte	Moderately loud	
Mezzo-piano	Moderately soft	
Mezza voce	(lit. Half voice.) Murmured	
Minore	Minor	
Misterioso	Mysterious	

TERM	TRANSLATION/EXPLANATION	ABBREVIATION
Mit (G)	With	
Moderato	Moderate time	
Moll (G)	Minor	
Molto	Much	
Morendo	Dying away	
Mosso Moto	Movement	
M.S. (E)	Manuscript	
Motet (E)	A sacred choral composition, usually unaccompanied	
Musical (E)	A modern dramatic musical production set for vocal soloists, chorus and orchestra. May contain some dialogue	
Nicht (G)	Not	
Nobilmente	Nobly	
Non	Not	
Non tanto	Not so much	
Non troppo	Not too much	
Obbligato	Must not be left out	
Octet	A piece for eight people	
Opera	A play set to music for vocalists and orchestra	
Oratorio	A biblical story set to music for vocal soloists, chorus and orchestra	
Overture	An orchestral introduction to an opera, oratorio, musical or show	
Parlante/ Parlando	(lit. Speaking.) To be sung in a style, using the natural inflections of speech	
Passionato	Passionately	
Pausa	Pause	
Perdendosi	Dying away	
Pesante	Heavily	
Piano	Soft	
Pianissimo	Very soft	
Piu	More	
Piu mosso	More movement	
Poco	A little	
Poco a poco	Little by little	
Poco meno mosso	A little less movement	

TERM	TRANSLATION/EXPLANATION	ABBREVIATION
Portamento	Gliding smoothly between notes	
Presto	Very fast	
Prestissimo	As fast as possible	
Primo	First	
Prima volta	First time	
Quasi	As if, almost, like	
Quasi recitativo	Like a recitative	
Rallentando	Gradually getting slower	Rall.
Ritardando	Gradually getting slower	Ritard.
Ritenuto	Held back, slower at once	Rit.
Recitative	A type of vocal writing that follows the natural rhythm patterns of speech	Recit.
Repeat (E)	Repeat	
Requiem	A mass for the dead, set to music	
Risoluto	Boldly	
Ritmico	Rhythmically	
Round (E)	A canon in unison for three or more voices, e.g. *Three blind mice*	
Rubato	(lit. Stolen.) The rhythm of a piece is stretched and broadened	
Ruhig (G)	Calm	
Scale	A sequence of notes in ascending, or descending pitch	
Scherzando	Playfully	
Schnell (G)	Fast	
Schneller (G)	Faster	
Segno	A sign; *see* Dal segno	
Segue	Carrying straight on	
Sehr (G)	Very	
Sempre	Always	
Senza	Without	
Sforzando	Forcing, accented	
Sforzato	Strongly accented	
Slentando	Gradually getting slower	
Smorzando	Dying away	
Soave	Gently	
Sonore	With a full tone	
Sopra	Above	
Sospirando	Sighing	

TERM	TRANSLATION/EXPLANATION	ABBREVIATION
Sostenuto	Sustained	
Sotto voce	Murmured	
Spiritoso	Spirited	
Staccato	Short and detached	
Strepitoso	Boisterous	
Stringendo	Gradually faster	
Subito	Suddenly	
Tacit	Silent, cut out	
Tempo	Speed	
Teneramente	Tenderly	
Tenuto	Held	
Transpose	To read or write down music in a higher or lower key than that in which it was written	
Tranquillo	Tranquil	
Traurig (G)	Sadly	
Troppo	Too much	
Tutti	All	
Vibrato	Vibrating	
Vivace	Quickly and lively	
Vivo	Animated	
Voce	Voice	
Volti Subito	Turn the page quickly	V.S.
Wenig (G)	Little	
Zart (G)	Delicate	

— USEFUL ADDRESSES —

Association of Professional Music Therapists
38 Pierce Lane
Fulbourn Cambridgeshire
CB1 5DL
Tel: 01223 880377

Barbershop Quartet Singing in America
6315 Third Avenue
Kenosha
Wisconsin 53143-5199
USA
Tel: 0101 414 653 8440
See also Sweet Adelines

Beamish Hall Summer School
University of Durham
44 Old Elvet Durham
DH1 3HN
Tel: 0191 374 3721
Opportunities to develop vocal skills.

Birmingham Conservatoire
Birmingham Polytchnic
Paradise Place Birmingham
B3 3HG
Tel: 0121 331 5901/5902

Black Music Association UK
146 Manor Park Road
London
NW10 4JP
Tel: 0181 961 4857

The British Association of Barbershop Singers
Little Orchard
Manor Road
Claybrook Magna
Leics
LE17 5AY
Tel: 01455 209555

The British Federation of Youth Choirs
37 Frederick Street
Loughborough
Leics
LE11 3BH
Tel: 01509 211664
Vocal workshops and masterclasses, etc.

British Kodaly Academy
Mary Place
11 Cotland Acres
Pentland Park
Redhill
Surrey
RH1 6LB
Tel: 01737 242974

**British Society for Music
  Therapy**
69 Avondale Avenue
East Barnet
Herts
EN4 8NB
Tel: 0181 368 8879

The British Voice Association
77b Abbey Road
London
NW8 0EA
Tel: 0171 328 1015
Offers demonstrations and work-
  shops to reveal how best vocal
  practice may be achieved.

British Youth Opera
South Bank Polytechnic
Manor House Branch
58 Clapham Common North Side
London
SW4 9RZ
Tel: 0171 738 2725
Singers should be over 21. Auditions
  held late January, early
  February. Many areas through-
  out the country have council
  sponsored, amateur opera groups.
  Contact your local council for
  details.

**Canford Summer School of
  Music**
5 Bushey Close
Old Barn Lane
Kenley

Surrey
CR8 5AU
Tel: 0181 660 4766

**Chest, Heart and Stroke
  Association – Scotland**
Head Office
65 North Castle Street
Edinburgh
EH2 3LT
Tel: 0131 225 6963
See also British Society for Music
  Therapy

**Chest, Heart and Stroke
  Association – Northern
  Ireland**
21 Dublin Road Belfast
BT12 7FJ
Tel: 0232 320184
See also British Society for Music
  Therapy and Stroke Association,
  London

Chetham's School of Music
Long Millgate Manchester
M3 1SB
Tel: 0161 834 9644

Choir Schools' Association
Wells Cathedral Choir School
15 The Liberty
Wells
Somerset
BA5 2SP
Tel: 01749 672117

**The City of Leeds College of
  Music**
Cookridge Street
Leeds
LS2 8BH
Tel: 0113 2452069

COMA
Contemporary Music-Making for
  Amateurs
13 Wellington Way

Bow London
E3 4NE
Tel: 0181 980 1527

Concerts From Scratch
PO Box No 1667
Bath
BA3 6YE

Curwen Institute
17 Primrose Avenue
Chadwell Heath
Romford
Essex
RM6 4QB
Tel: 0181 599 8230
Annual summer and Christmas
courses, also one-day, weekend
and other occasional courses.

**Dartington International
Summer School**
Dartington Hall
Devon
TQ9 6DE
Tel: 01803 865988

**Division of Music and
Performing Arts**
Anglia Polytechnic University
East Road
Cambridge
CB1 1PT
Tel: 01223 63271

English National Opera
London Coliseum
St Martin's Lane
London
WC2N 4ES
Tel: 0171 836 0111

English Touring Opera
W121 Westminster Business Square
Durham Street
London
SE11 5JH
Tel: 0171 820 1131

Gilbert and Sullivan Society
31a Kenmere Gardens
Wembley
Middlesex
HA0 1TD

Glyndebourne Touring Opera
Lewes
East Sussex
BN8 5UU
Tel: 01273 812321

**Guildhall School of Music and
Drama**
Barbican
London
EC2Y 8DT
Tel: 0171 628 2571
Guildhall also runs various external
courses.

Hereford Summer School
27 Goldsmith Road
Kings Heath
Birmingham
B14 7EH
Tel: 0121 443 4479

**Incorporated Society of
Musicians**
10 Stratford Place
London
W1N 9AE
Tel: 0171 629 4413

London College of Music
Polytechnic of West London
St Mary's Road
Ealing
London
W5 5RF
Tel: 0181 579 5000

National Opera Studio
c/o Morley College
61 Westminster Bridge Road
London
SE1 7HT
Tel: 0171 928 6833

National Youth Choir
PO Box 67
Holmfirth
West Yorkshire
HD7 1GQ
Tel: 01484 687023

Nordoff-Robbins Music Therapy Centre
2 Lissenden Gardens
London
NW5 1PP
Tel: 0171 267 4496

Opera Factory
8a The Leathermarket
Weston Street
London
SE1
Tel: 0171 378 1029

Opera North
Grand Theatre
46 New Briggate
Leeds
LS1 6NU
Tel: 0113 2439999

Roehampton Institute
Senate House
Roehampton Lane
London
SW15 5PU
Tel: 0181 878 8117
One year full-time diploma in Music Therapy, for music graduates.

Royal Academy of Music
York Gate
Marylebone Road
London
NW1 5HT
Tel: 0171 935 5461

Royal College of Music
Prince Consort Road
London
SW7 2BS
Tel: 0171 589 3643

Royal Northern College of Music
124 Oxford Road
Manchester
M13 9RD
Tel: 0161 273 6283

Royal Opera House
Covent Garden
London
WC2E 9DD
Tel: 0171 240 1200

Royal Scottish Academy of Music and Drama
11 Renfrew Street
Glasgow
G2 3DB
Tel: 0141 332 4101

The Royal School of Church Music (RSCM)
Addington Place
Croydon
Surrey
CR9 5AD
Tel: 0181 654 7676
RSCM also runs a Sing Aloud Choral Scheme for junior members, aged 7½–13½.

Scottish Opera
39 Elmbank Crescent
Glasgow
G2 4PT
Tel: 0141 248 4567

Sing for Pleasure
25 Fryerning Lane
Ingatestone
Essex
CM4 0DD
Tel: 01277 353691

South Yorkshire Opera
1 Broad Lane
Sheffield
South Yorkshire
S1 4BS
Tel: 0114 2754879

Grand opera productions in rep' in
summer season, operetta in
winter seasons, one-night
concerts, etc.

The Stroke Association
CHSA House
Whitecross Street
London
EC1Y 8JJ
Tel: 0171 490 7999
See also British Society for Music
Therapy
Sing-along tapes available.

Sweet Adelines International
PO Box 470168
Tulsa
OK 74147
USA
An educational organisation
promoting four-part harmony,
barbershop style, for women.

Trinity College of Music
11–13 Mandeville Place
London
W1M 6AQ
Tel: 0171 935 5773

**Welsh College of Music and
Drama**
Castle Grounds
Cardiff
CF1 3ER
Tel: 01222 342854

**Yorkshire College of Music and
Drama**
Shire Oak Road
Headingley
Leeds
LS6 2DD
Tel: 0113 2751232

For further listings of music organisations, competitions, scholarships and
education, refer to the British Music Yearbook, which can be found in the
reference section of most libraries.

—— BIBLIOGRAPHY ——

Alvin, J   *Music Therapy for the Autistic Child*; Oxford University Press, 1978.

Campbell, P Shehan   *Lessons from the World*; Schirmer Books, 1991.

Croiza, C   *The Singer as Interpreter*; Gollancz, 1989.

Dewhurst-Maddock, O   *The Book of Sound Therapy*; Gaia Books, 1993.

Haasemann, F and Jordan, J   *Group Vocal Techniques*; Hinshaw/Elkin, 1991.

Harker, D   *Fakesong*; Open University Press, 1985. (Shows the means by which Folksong has been preserved.)

Husler, F and Rodd-Marling, Y   *Singing: the Physical Nature of the Vocal Organ*; Faber, 1965.

Legge, A   *The Art of Auditioning*; Rhinegold, 1988.

Herwitt, G   *How to Sing*; Elm Tree/EMI Music, 1978.

Hewitt, J   *Teach Yourself Relaxation*; Hodder and Stoughton, 1985.

Hines, J   *Great Singers on Great Singing*; Gollancz, 1983.

Kaplan, M   *Barbershopping: Musical and Social Harmony*; Associated University Presses, 1993.

Manen, L   *The Art of Singing*; Faber, 1974.

Newham, P   *The Singing Cure*; Rhinegold, 1993.

Rao, D   *We will Sing*; Boosey and Hawkes, 1993.